Adventures Over Sixty

Gail

Also by Gail Boulanger

Life Goes On: Losing, letting go and living again

Gail Boulanger

Adventures Over Sixty

notch
hill
books

Nanoose Bay, BC

Library and Archives Canada Cataloguing in Publication

Boulanger, Gail, 1947-
    Adventures over sixty / Gail Boulanger.

Also issued in electronic format.
ISBN 978-0-9730802-3-0

    1. Aging--Psychological aspects.　I. Title.

BF724.55.A35B68 2012   155.67   C2012-903272-7

Edited by Susan Mayse

Book Layout and Design by Paula Gaube, Editworks Online

Photograph of Gail Boulanger by Bill Perison
Front cover photo Copyright © iStockPhoto.com / Lukasphoto

Published by
Notch Hill Books
PO Box 252, Nanoose Bay, B.C. Canada
V9P 9J9

www.gailboulanger.com

Printed in Canada by Friesens

To Lou

Ingenious, courageous, wholehearted.

Our adventure continues.

CONTENTS

Part III
Tacking

Part IV
Anchors in the Wind

ACKNOWLEDGEMENTS

OUR LIVES ARE MADE UP of moments that we weave together into stories to make sense of who we are and our place in the world. *Adventures Over Sixty* would not exist without the moments I've shared with special people, and some of these moments now grace these pages.

"Thank you" barely conveys my deep gratitude for the many family, friends, mentors, colleagues, coaching clients and neighbours who touch my heart and light my path.

Some people have passed out of my life, but I still bask in the glow of their gifts. I am grateful that I can share moments from their lives to inspire and inform: my mother, Margie; my father, Ken; my aunt Joan; my grand-uncle Pete and my father-in-law, Gus; Mrs. Dandurand; Mrs. Lukes; my first hospice client, Maria; my first-year university English professor, William J. Goede; and my friend and colleague Bev Abbey. I've changed the names of some others to protect their privacy. I thank them all for their kindness, generosity and wisdom.

Several people graciously gave permission for me to share their inspiring anecdotes. Darin Abbey, thank you for calling me with Bev's greeting and kindly consenting to be part of my stories. I look forward to more invigorating walks in the woods. Bob Drummond, thank you for clarifying the details of your journey with Bev in her final months and for permission to honour her in this book. Peter Mason, congratulations on walking 10,000 steps a day for over five years, an amazing accomplishment that can motivate us all. Thank you also for proudly telling me of the equally inspiring walking adventures of your sister, Brenda Simeoni. Brenda, welcome to *Adventures Over Sixty*. Thank you for letting me share some of your story with my readers. Eleanor Bell, thank you for your thoughtful touch and a single, simple word: "Welcome." Maggie, what a privilege it was to witness your spontaneous gesture of human kindness. Thank you!

Eve Flynn, manager of Nanoose Place Community Centre, and Lesley Seselja of Nanoose Business Services Directory, you are both a joy to work with. Eve, thank you for your flexibility, which makes my workshops possible. Lesley, thank you for your creative design work.

Bent Sorensen, we're so glad that you're too young to retire. Thank you for generously sharing your knowledge and permitting me to extol your gifts to my readers. Anne Duggan, I appreciate your zest for life and entrepreneurial spirit. It does my heart good to know you're actively advocating for seniors in our community. We also benefit from the integrity and experience of Jon Cockcroft, hearing aid specialist. Thank you, Jon, for educating me about the realities of hearing loss; you are a patient teacher and a great adviser for anyone adjusting to diminished hearing. Rollie, you are a special brother-in-law. I am always grateful for your warm Prairie welcome and loyal sense of family. Thank you particularly for the story of the shoes.

Dear Aunt Edna, thank you for your gracious hospitality and passionate love of life. I greatly appreciate our professional collegial relationship and your unstinting support for my work. I thank both you and Al for encouraging me to republish *Life Goes On: Losing, letting go and living again.* Eileen, I am most grateful for your welcoming hugs and endearing eternal optimism. Thank you for letting me share a sliver of your rich, long life, best captured in your own book, written by your dear friends James Hawkins and Sheila Swanson: *Eileen Wilson – Still Dancing at Ninety: The Biography of an Extraordinary Ordinary Woman.*

Barbara Rinehart, thank you for inviting me into the unknown and breaking me out of my comfortable cocoon; our adventures always enlighten and encourage me. Audrey Chowdhury, thank you for our many enlightening talks across the miles between here and Wisconsin, and for travelling to Nanoose Bay to share your wisdom and expertise with SoulCollage participants. Erin McGrath, my friend, thank you for your assistance, support and flexibility. I admire your down-to-earth common sense and discernment and look forward to more walking and talking adventures. Trudy Boyle, we have walked many a crooked mile together over the past thirty-five years. I appreciate your encouragement and enthusiasm for my every venture. You inspire all of us who know you with your optimistic resilience, grace and dignity. I am eternally grateful for our enduring friendship.

Lynda Ishim, you are one determined, courageous senior! Your solitary cross-Canada driving trip is a true inspiration. Thank you for letting me share it with my readers. Bill Perison, what a superbly patient tai chi teacher you are! I extend my heartfelt gratitude for our mutually clarifying and creative walks around Westwood Lake. Thank you for listening and for permitting me to tell about your tenacious journey with meditation and tai chi. Mickey, we have come such a long way together! Your resilience, tenacity and wholehearted engagement with life shine like a beacon for family, friends, colleagues and students. You are a true heroine, and I am ever grateful for our friendship.

Thank you, Cousin Rose, for welcoming us to your Quadra Island retreat, feeding us generous gourmet meals, and taking us on walking and oyster-collecting expeditions. Above all, I am grateful for your story of determination and recovery. My brother, Ferg, and sister-in-law, Joy, our Quadra Island jaunt wouldn't have been half so much fun without your cozy dining table and delicious repast. It was a summer sojourn to remember.

My stalwart siblings, Ferg and Liz, keepers of family history, deserve my warmest thanks for stories remembered and birthdays never forgotten. Carlene, my dear niece, thank you for your interest, enthusiasm and support. As my own adventures over sixty continue, I'm comforted to know that, should I again take a nasty fall or sprain my wrist, you're nearby with sound professional sports-injury advice.

My son Marty and my daughter-in-law Kathy, I am so glad your car developed a roof-top whine that needed Lou's diagnosis; what a difference that experience made to our lives, and what a great story it contributed! Thank you both for your generosity. My son Joey, thank you for all the time you spent searching for the perfect bells to enhance my workshops and, along with my daughter-in-law Lynsey, thank you for your constant encouragement with all my writing and workshop endeavours. Lynsey, thank you for assisting me with workshops; your sensitivity to participants ensured the days flowed well from beginning to end. Knowing that the four of you are as close as the phone or a two-hour drive brightens my every day.

Page and Michael Ough, my open-hearted, energetic friends, thank you for your inclusive generosity and support. Michael, thank you for respecting my fear of off-leash dogs and telling me about your dog, Boutrous, a tale that led to so many other rich meetings. Page, my friend and kindred spirit, your hard work and dedication to your art constantly inspire me. Thank you for truly understanding my ongoing doubts. Your empathic listening means the world to me and never fails to lift my spirits.

I am indebted to the many experienced professionals who provided input and guidance at various stages of my writing journey. Brooke Warner, you threw me a lifeline when I was drowning, and I'll always be grateful. Thank you for coaching me out of the swamp. I send virtual thanks every single day to Margaret Rode, website wizard, who created and maintains my website. Thank you, Margaret, for your attention to detail, your quiet patience with my endless questions and your lightning attention to my constant changes.

Trish Rorison, thank you for the hours you spent ferreting out hard-to-find information and for your extensive, impeccable research. Thank you, Kari Magnuson, proofreader par excellence, for your attention to even the smallest points of punctuation and syntax. Paula Gaube, book designer, thank you. Your keen, artistic eye enhanced *Life Goes On: Losing, letting go and living again*, and brought depth and beauty to *Adventures Over Sixty*.

Susan Mayse, author, mentor, editor and friend, you have again helped me transform a dream into a living book. You rattle my cage until I produce gold nuggets that you help me forge into shining sentences. Thank you for your wisdom, vision and insistence that I lighten up, laugh and tell stories.

Thank you, one and all!

Gail Boulanger
June 2012

Preface

I AM AN ISLANDER WITH Prairie roots. As a child I loved running barefoot through fields of wild purple crocus and yellow buffalo beans. Some days I would lie on my back, gazing at the vast sky and building castles in the clouds. Other days I was more down to earth. One year the city dug up, levelled and paved our road. The dirty, yellow heavy equipment—left idle overnight—was better than any jungle gym. The foreign smell of machine grease and oil mixed with dirt was tantalizing, and I easily scrambled up the tractor lugs. I loved climbing into the cab and sitting on the cracked, black vinyl seat to pretend I was driving. I had a commanding view. I was in charge, and it felt great.

I moved to Victoria when I was eighteen, and the sea drew me like a magnet. I needed space to breathe. As I walked Dallas Road from Clover Point to the end of the Ogden Point breakwater and back, I dreamed of setting sail. On calm days and nights, I would look across at the blinking lights of Port Angeles and wonder about that distant shore in another country. I liked nothing better than being on the breakwater in a raging storm as seas crashed on the concrete wall, sending salt spray up and over the top. I laughed out loud, soaked from head to toe. It was invigorating, and I felt alive.

That's how it feels to be in my mid-sixties: vigorous and alive. I have a commanding view, and I'm in charge. I no longer have to ask anyone else for permission. I no longer have anything left to prove. I can walk barefoot in the sand to my heart's content or get drenched in the rain. I can wear my pearls with sandals and jeans every day if I've a mind. It gives me a giddy feeling, all this freedom!

Although I've happily shed my youth, I must admit that I am a bit surprised that I've arrived on this distant shore. I've heard other seniors—family members, friends, clients and neighbours—also express surprise at getting to this age. We all agree that it feels like a considerable accomplishment, and the beckoning lights ahead intrigue us.

When I have questions, I write. I write to know and understand myself and my world. I decided to write a book to explore "adventures over sixty" and get a feel for the new territory yet to discover.

Will you join me? Together we can embark on new learning experiences that promise to inspire, inform and—above all—invigorate.

Part I

Getting Underway

1

Yearning

I WAS RESTLESS IN THE autumn months leading up to my fifty-ninth birthday. Had I not shredded all my journals, I could give you a detailed description of exactly what I was and wasn't doing. When I'm restless, I walk more miles than I normally do through my neighbourhood, in the woods and on nearby beaches; it seems I'm waiting for answers to arrive on the wind. I find solace in the seagulls' raucous cries and in the iodine-tinged smell of seaweed mingled with salt that lingers along driftwood-strewn shores. I squelch kelp bulbs, kick up bits of jetsam and make half-hearted attempts to skip rocks across the water. Most sink.

And when answers don't arrive on the wind, I usually eat too many cashews and fresh dates and drink too much hot chocolate with marshmallows. I make cookies—my favourites include ultimate chocolate-chip cookies, cheese-raisin nibbles and crunchy peanut-butter bars—and I eat them and give them away. I do some of my best thinking while walking or baking. My husband, Lou, would tell you that I think too much, but he does enjoy the aroma of cookies coming out of the oven.

That autumn I felt adrift like a ship without a rudder. Questions flooded my mind. What was life about over sixty? What did my life say? More important, and perhaps more difficult to answer, what did I want it to say? When I took part in conversations and heard myself talking, I seriously questioned my opinions. I felt as though I no longer knew what I really thought or what really mattered. I was confused.

Not surprisingly, one day I woke up wondering what I really think and what I really want to say. So began my quest to find my own voice, discover what I think at this time in my life and develop the courage to put my own ideas out in the world. I devoured thought-provoking philosophical books, particularly books on vibrant aging. I came to believe that the journey in our second half of life must stretch us and encourage us to grow so that we don't allow ourselves to drift and stagnate. I found it disconcerting that I questioned much of the academic foundation upon which I'd built my thinking, but a tiny seed of excitement now began to take root.

December 2006 marked the end of my formal relationship with psychology; I had enrolled in my first university psychology course in September 1966. For forty years, in one role or another, I had actively pursued knowledge and the understanding of human nature. For twenty-five years I'd maintained a private practice in counselling, consulting and psychotherapy. It was rich, rewarding work that I dearly loved, but it was time to explore new horizons. On December 7 I saw my last client. On December 8—my fifty-ninth birthday—my office phone line ceased and I took my degrees off the wall.

Planning an extended sabbatical, I designated this my peaceful "year in the woods" to read, reflect and write as Henry David Thoreau did when he wrote *Walden; or Life in the Woods*. What actually happened was conflict and chaos.

Our house renovation started in early February. From the moment our back deck was demolished until mid-August, the renovation consumed virtually every waking moment. Our temporary kitchen was scattered around the dining room, laundry room and garage. Plastic sheathing, draped from ceiling to floor, failed to contain the lung-choking dust that seeped in everywhere as old walls came down and new ones rose. Drywall dust hung in the air like a fog. Construction workers wandered in and out, leaving a trail of dust and debris in their wake. It was actually a relief to work outside in the fresh air, moving our two-cord woodpile three times, log by log, from one corner of our yard to another. To add to our misery, Lou and I foolishly agreed to do all the cleanup, and although this saved us thousands of dollars, it strained our relationship almost to the breaking point.

This was not a peaceful year in the woods. I had no privacy, no quiet time and no peace. By the end of August I was exhausted, soul-weary and mind-numb.

As the long, hot summer gave way to cool September breezes, sanity returned. One night I had a dream: I was trying to fly but

I couldn't get off the ground. Nothing too complicated here; the clear message was that I was carrying too much baggage. I began shedding and shredding.

At first I just shredded my old journals, but the task soon took on a life of its own. When I finished, everything was gone: ten years of personal journals, five years of writing, old letters from my mother and father—both dead over twenty-five years—and childhood mementos from scrapbooks and yearbooks. All this I reduced to five bags of confetti. What a relief!

One memento that surfaced made me smile: my UH-5 crest and a four-inch piece of stiff material cut from a hat. I ran my hand over the colourful layers of felt, pried the hat material off the page and drifted back to my youth. When I was eleven in grade seven, I had four fast friends. We all went to an inner-city Catholic school and irreverently called ourselves the Un-Holy 5. Our unlikely crew consisted of two Hungarians, Big Louie (five foot eight) and Little Louie (five foot three); one tall, handsome, easy-going Italian nicknamed Nico; a wildly freckled, blue-eyed, blond Irish boy called John; and myself—"Sam," the lone girl. We were a close-knit if varied bunch, and I belonged.

We wore our matching hats, black-and-blue houndstooth fedoras, at a jaunty angle. Our crests contained our school colours of red and yellow on a black background. The U and H intertwined with the centred gold 5. Big Louie, our creative mastermind, lingered in front of any mirror he passed. He was also an exceptional chess player and checkmated my father on more than one occasion. We rode around on scooters owned by Big Louie and Little Louie. The most daring thing we ever did was siphon gas out of a car on Fourteenth Street in Southwest Calgary—only once—but got caught in the act and had to drop the jerry can and run for cover.

Mostly we hung out together at my house. For a few short months in our teens we smoked forbidden cigarettes, drank Coke, ate chips, played board games and listened to records. All too soon raging hormones disrupted our peace, and girlfriends appeared on the scene. Our group faded away as childhood groups do. It would be many long years before I again experienced such a warm sense of belonging.

Now, forty-six years later, here I was cutting up the crest that symbolized a happy childhood memory. We can learn much from the scraps we so carefully hoard. To better understand our history and ourselves, we need to take the scrapbooks down from the attic, turn the pages, touch the memories, wander along with them for a time, extract and retain the riches and release the rest. And in the process our lives begin, bit by bit, to make more sense. I now realize the shedding and shredding was an essential part of my process. On many levels I was letting go, saying goodbye to my younger body and my younger self, to say, "Hello and welcome" to my constantly changing older body and ever-evolving senior self.

When the five bags of confetti sat at my feet and I reflected on the task ahead, I felt an immense sense of freedom. I could begin again. Then I contacted Susan—writer, teacher, friend and sage—and asked her to create with me a writing course to improve my skills. When she agreed, I was over the moon. Together we walked the labyrinth at Queenswood, a retreat centre near Victoria on Vancouver Island. Later, as we strolled among stately oak and gnarled arbutus, a majestic eight-point stag crossed our path to browse on low-hanging branches. We stood stock-still, cherishing the sight of this magnificent animal. He turned his massive head our way and held us spellbound with a penetrating gaze from his deep brown eyes. That night the stag appeared in my dreams. Standing on the forest edge, he invited me to climb aboard. I felt called to the quest to find my voice—a new voice to carry me into my golden years.

For as long as I can remember, my voice has been that of a helper and protector of others. I grew into, lived and breathed the roles of daughter, sister, student, wife, mother, friend and therapist. I took all my roles and responsibilities seriously, and like so much baggage, they weighed me down. Unlike my papers, they weren't easily shed, nor did they need to be. What I did need, however, was to reassess all my roles, shake off those that no longer fit and redefine those that did.

This yearning to make major changes in our lives may come cloaked in any number of disguises such as restlessness, intense longing, heavy fatigue or severe depression. In *From Age-ing to Sage-ing: A Profound New Vision of Growing Older*, the respected rabbi and speaker Zalman Schachter-Shalomi wrote of feeling unbearably depressed as he approached his sixtieth birthday.

Plagued by questions, he particularly worried about ensuring that his senior years were of benefit rather than barren. He went on a forty-day retreat in Taos, New Mexico, and on his return set about learning the ins and outs of healthy aging. He shared his new-found enthusiasm in his book along with the details of courses he designed to encourage elders to become compassionate leaders in their communities.

I had the delight and privilege of meeting and hearing Zalman Schachter-Shalomi when he was eighty in the spring of 2004. I can still picture his bushy beard and wild hair as he ambled into the room wearing a long, loose khaki shirt over loose tan slacks, with his large feet snug in wool socks and worn sandals. He touched and greeted people as he moved through the room. Obviously much loved, he commanded our full attention as he comfortably seated himself in an overstuffed armchair on the dais. His eyes danced and sparkled as he entertained us with wise, humorous stories for well over an hour, and the laughter and applause suggested we could have happily listened to him for the entire afternoon. Clearly no longer depressed, he had turned his extra years into a gift for himself and his community.

My own goal is the same: to invite senior family members, friends, neighbours and all others to enthusiastically embrace growing older and joyously share what we have learned along life's bumpy road.

Many of us feel that one particular age has great significance; it's a milestone. As that age approaches—or the decade we are in recedes—we may feel an urge to celebrate or do something drastic: run or cycle a marathon, quit an unsatisfactory job, move from one end of the country to the other or even out of country, or leave an unworkable relationship. We may feel compelled to complete a dream left hanging in our youth such as going to university. For some of us the milestone year is when we turn thirty or forty or fifty, and that shocks us out of complacency. It reminds us that years are passing and we're growing older.

Sixty or sixty-five is significant for our generation; until recently in most jobs and professions, mandatory retirement loomed on the horizon. Forced retirement is quickly disappearing, but at that age many of us will change jobs or stop paid work altogether. As we embrace our extra years, we want to continue to nurture our mind, body and spirit by remaining mentally alert, physically agile and enthusiastic. One of the best ways to do this is to embark on a daring adventure, consciously seeking answers to age-old questions and intentionally challenging ourselves to change and grow.

Chaos, confusion and conflict attend all such adventures. We may wander down many different paths before we step onto one that will lead us forward. It helps greatly to see value in all roads travelled and all experiences gained; no effort is wasted.

My own adventure that I set for myself in my early sixties has been the reading, thinking and rethinking, writing and rewriting that it took to create this book. It is my marathon, both daring and daunting. It is exhilarating. When it is complete, I expect to know what I believe at this time in my life, and I trust that those now well-tilled beliefs will enrich my future. It will be a bonus if I can express my ideas clearly and invitingly for all readers. Stories beg to be told; contributions to my community give meaning and purpose to my life; and my nature is to share the excitement of new discoveries.

My parents both died too young. They were not yet sixty-three, tired and disheartened. I don't want to die that way, and that desire fuels my quest. An average lifespan of eighty-two years adds up to 30,000 days, an idea popularized by Gregg Krech, editor of *Thirty Thousand Days: A Journal for Purposeful Living*. Barring unforeseen accidents or debilitating health problems, I can look forward to at least another possible 6,640 days. Time is precious, and I want each day to count. I devote my attention to achieving and maintaining a life-enhancing balance between solitary activities, precious time spent with kindred spirits and stimulating group activities. This is my ongoing creative enterprise—an adventure.

2

ALONENESS

TODAY'S BLEAK, DRIZZLY DECEMBER WEATHER suits my mood. This morning I learned that I require cataract surgery on my right eye and eventually on my left. My doctor clearly and concisely explained the process and answered my questions. His pleasant assistant was efficient as she gathered more information and entered my name into the system. I am grateful for excellent medical care but sad that my eyes are more compromised as I get older. Since I also have glaucoma, cataract surgery may help reduce the pressure on my optic nerve. I remind myself that this is good news.

I need to be alone with all this information and let go of my illusion of perfect eyesight. It is no longer perfect; in fact it hasn't been for many years. I had perfect eyesight for forty-five years, while my older brother, Ferg, and younger sister, Liz, both needed strong glasses as young children. I've used reading glasses for twenty years and take them for granted. I'd also taken it for granted that my eyes would remain much the same—needing only reading glasses—till old age. The cataracts have grown steadily for six years, complicated no doubt by the glaucoma that my doctor discovered two years ago. I grieved when I gave up vigorous length-swimming, having intuitively decided I would no longer wear protective goggles—too much pressure—or put my face in the water—too much risk of infection. Now I'm grieving again.

When my surgery day arrives, Lou will drive me into town and drop me off, returning later to pick me up. If I ask, he'll stay and keep me company until I go up for surgery, but he hates hospitals. A few close friends would willingly offer the same support. It's best if I wait alone, though. I need to be able to pay absolute attention to myself, ensure that I listen to all the necessary instructions, meditate and relax; for that I must be alone. I don't want chatty conversation and I don't want to be distracted. I want to remain focused, concentrating on the task ahead.

Aloneness to me means altogether at one with myself, and this state of mind is not lonely. On the contrary, it is whole, complete and—at least for the moment—nurturing. It's not that I don't reach out for support and assistance. I do. After I spend time alone, I call my friends and talk to them. When I open my mouth to tell them a sad tale, usually my tears begin to flow. My friends listen, empathize and hug me virtually or in person. And I gratefully accept their compassion and comfort.

After all these years, I wear solitude like a comfortable old jacket. It is a familiar friend with whom I've had both painful and exciting adventures. My first accidental experience of safety in aloneness may have led me to withdraw into myself when hurt, humiliated or injured. Over time, similar experiences entrenched this pattern. Now I seek aloneness in times of trouble; only once I regain my equilibrium do I reach out for further support.

One cold, bleak day close to sixty years ago I suffered a terrible shock. The school bell clanged, calling the children in from the playground to start a typical school day. St. Angeles Catholic School in Northeast Calgary occupied a cold, cavernous building that smelled of leftover tuna sandwiches and mouldy cheese. Like many Catholic schools in the fifties, it was run by nuns in long, flowing black habits with a white band stretched tightly across the forehead. Even the smallest nun loomed large and intimidating in her billowing black gown.

My patchy memory throws up a dark picture of a particularly tall apparition standing over me. Mother Dominica grabbed my shoulder and hauled me up in front of the class for talking in line. I was only five and in grade one. The talking I don't remember, but I do remember her powerful arm raised, strap in hand, as she brought it down with a resounding smack. I remember the sting of harsh leather on my small hands and tears springing to my eyes. First one hand, then the other, turned a bright, cruel pink. So did my face, but the other children's laughter was quickly stifled by a scowl and a stern word. I had never before been struck. I was shocked speechless, which was just as well.

Soon I was scrambling alone up the hill behind the school, heading home. It was time, or so I thought. I called back to my friend Danny, but he wasn't coming, and all the other children were still running around on the playground. I didn't understand, but I kept on climbing as if in a trance. Once I crested the hill, I was soon out of sight of the school. I was alone—safe. It was very quiet. I walked slowly home through a field, down a couple of blocks, around the high school playground, along a few more streets—passing the neighbourhood grocery store—then around the corner and past Danny's house to my own yard. I went in the back door, and a startled Mrs. Lukes greeted me. It wasn't even lunchtime! I'd escaped at the first opportunity, at mid-morning recess. I was hurt and I headed home.

Mrs. Lukes was our tall, buxom, kind-hearted babysitter, who always smelled of lavender. Every morning she arrived with a flourish to look after my baby sister while my older brother and I went to school and Mum and Dad went to work. Mrs. Lukes made scrumptious, warm, white dinner rolls and plump, sticky cinnamon buns dripping with syrup. Her love encompassed all of us. That day was no exception. Mrs. Lukes gathered me in her arms and comforted me as I told her what had happened, and I imagine she bristled with indignation that anyone would hurt one of "her babies." She phoned my mother at work. Mum was equally as angry—at the nun, not at me. I was allowed to stay home for the rest of the day and given the special privilege of watching an afternoon television program called *Carousel* on our black-and-white TV. The movie that day was *The Spiral Staircase*. I can picture an elegantly gowned woman standing alone at the top of a spiral staircase—but that's all I remember.

The powerful lessons I learned that day remain with me still. I could walk away from a toxic environment; I've always found freedom and comfort in that. Being alone was preferable to being hit or playing with children who laughed at me; the safety of wide-open spaces, in fields or on the ocean, soothes my soul. I'd taken care of myself, and my family didn't punish me for that; in fact, I think Mum may have admired my unconscious temerity. I was, after all, her daughter. Mum could have insisted that Mrs. Lukes send me back to school in the afternoon, but she wasn't about to do that until she dealt with the school authorities, ensuring that such severe abuse would never again happen to her daughter.

That was the first time I walked home from school by myself; it wasn't the last. I was physically hurt by the strap and emotionally scarred by the entire experience, particularly the laughter of the other children. I began to spend more time alone. I fell in love with the freedom I felt out of doors. On my own I could dilly-dally and wander off the beaten path; I felt less constrained, more adventurous and free, than in a crowd. This remains true today. I'm fortunate never to have felt lonely, and I don't remember ever feeling afraid when I've been alone indoors or out. If these blessings come from my strapping experience, I'm grateful.

Other people tell me that being alone can be frightening and lonely. It's one thing to seek solitude or be naturally drawn to it, but quite another thing to face it through changing life circumstances.

My friend Lynda would be the first to admit that she always surrounded herself with people. She made sure she was never alone; it was easy because she genuinely loves people—the more the merrier—and she's a true extrovert. A petite, vivacious woman who lights up a room with her love of life, Lynda can galvanize any group into action with her boundless energy. She's the one who always makes the new person in the group feel welcome.

Lynda and her husband, Collin, were well into their sixties when he died after a lengthy and painful battle with cancer. She then faced, for the first time in her life, the none-too-pleasant prospect of living alone. But never the shrinking violet, she confronted her fears about both silence and solitude. She would drive alone across Canada from Vancouver Island on the west coast to Newfoundland on the east coast, a longer drive than from Seattle to New York City. Lynda embarked on a daring adventure to rediscover her courage.

Shortly before she left in the spring of 2006, I ran into her in a local doughnut shop. She was practising going into a restaurant and having a cup of coffee on her own. Just imagine that tentative beginning—coupled with the fear she later told me she felt as she pulled out of her driveway—not only the first morning but many mornings in the first month of her adventure. The next day she was going to Vancouver to get more familiar with her new GPS. I shook my head in admiration of her grit.

Lynda returned from her three-month cross-country trek confident in her ability to live and navigate on her own. We met recently in her cozy condo, which was gaily decorated for the season with figurines, red velvet ribbons and a perfect petite Christmas tree. She readily shared some of her insights. Lynda learned the difference between being alone and being lonely, and although she's now sometimes lonely, she regularly chooses to be alone. She delights in silence and solitude, two states of being that she previously feared and avoided. She now relishes returning home from her travels and sinking into the comfort of her own space. Lynda lives alone and thrives.

Lynda would agree, I am sure, that solitude creates an environment in which we can pay attention to our own voice. Only when we're alone does the cacophony of others' voices fade and our own quiet voice emerge from the recesses of our mind. Making alone time lets us hear ourselves think and, more important, know what we think. Solitude is like an underground hot spring where ideas bubble up and burst on the surface of our mind.

Lou works in solitude in his shop, always building or manufacturing something that enhances our life. Recently he built me a sound box. I am technologically challenged—believe me, this is no exaggeration. Turning down the ringer on my office phone and quieting an incoming message on the answering machine was too complicated by half! But it's an essential courtesy to ensure clients aren't interrupted when they're sharing their stories. After tearful sessions when he showed me the many annoying buttons I had to press to silence the phone, my creative husband suggested another solution. I bought a beautiful cream-coloured box with a magical dragonfly on the easy-to-lift lid; Lou insulated it with soft grey foam—ironically, the same foam that insulates the diesel engine on our boat—and cut out a perfect slot for the phone and handset. Now, before a client arrives, I deposit the phone in the sound box, add two insulated foam layers and replace the dragonfly lid. Blessed peace!

I know, understand and cherish gifts discovered in solitude. Solitude is as essential to our emotional well-being as air is for our physical well-being. The older we get, the more times of solitude we will encounter.

All of us benefit from solitary times in nature. Will you join me?

Early mornings are cool, and I love the fragrance of dew-damp grass. As I walk, here and there I catch the aroma of coffee, signalling other early risers. Some mornings I receive the gift of sunrise backlighting the clouds that colour the sky pale pink, yellow and turquoise like an ever-changing kaleidoscope. I admire the trees and catch the flash of a furry, light-brown rabbit bounding between blackberry bushes. This morning two women are running alone in different directions; one has a beautiful tan boxer named Ace who runs regally alongside her. We all nod and carry on our way. We cherish our solitude. I arrive home refreshed and energized, ready for another day.

3

Silence invites reflection

YESTERDAY A LITTLE BIRD BUMPED into my window and flew away as if to say, "Get up from your computer and come outside!" And so I did and was showered with blessings.

It was a cool, overcast day, and I wandered down by a local pond where I regularly walk. The red-winged blackbirds usually sing from the swaying tops of the bulrushes, but today they flew about and up into the trees. I stopped to watch one that seemed particularly agitated. His tail rose and fell each time he made a clicking sound, reminding me of how our resident squirrel jerks her tail when she voices her displeasure at being ousted from my bird feeder. It dawned on me that I could be near a nest; the birds might be trying to draw me away. I walked on past.

Then I listened to the frogs croaking and watched two mallard ducks land with a swish on the pond, their emerald-green heads shining in the grey day. I counted five deer: three bucks with their fuzz-covered antlers just beginning to sprout and two does munching on grass. The delicate scent of wild roses drew me over to their thorny bush, and I put my nose right up to the damp, pale pink petals to drink in the exquisite perfume.

Later that day it poured with rain pounding on my office window; then suddenly it stopped. I love the smell after a heavy rainfall, so I stepped outside, and for a moment the silence was absolute. All was still. The quiet was awe-inspiring; nature is rarely still or silent. A moment of awe is rare and precious, a gift that quickly passes. I was grateful that I stopped long enough to listen.

Silence encourages reflection and contemplation; it smoothes out the wrinkles in our lives. My writing sanctuary is silent, with only the hum of the computer and the click of keys when I type. Ideas spring forth in silence, take root in the compost of my mind, mature and eventually blossom into the written word.

In the spring of 2010 I attended a retreat with twelve other women; it included one full day and two nights spent in silence. We came from near and far, each for different reasons, and we left behind the noise and demands of our daily lives. We came together in a wilderness setting for inspiration, renewal and self-discovery led by three wise women elders: Seena, Mariabruna and Miriam. We met on a high plateau surrounded by immense trees in the hills above Los Gatos, California, where an old, white mission building nestled in the trees above a deep gorge. Nearby were a two-storey, white stucco residence and a large, modern, glass-fronted dining room. Rustic cabins perched around the periphery of the wide-open spaces.

Friday late afternoon and evening we spent getting to know each other and sharing our first meal together. We later had an opportunity to express our excitement and anxiety about spending time in silence. I was surprised at the degree of fear and apprehension I heard. Two or three women joked that they were afraid to be alone with their thoughts. This was my first silent retreat, but I relish silence, and their comments reminded me that this is not the norm. In our culture we don't value silence highly. In fact for many people it's a rare experience.

Saturday morning began in silence as we stretched and breathed our way into the day. We had our first meal together in silence, which was fascinating. Eating in silence gave me a whole new appreciation for food. I chewed more thoroughly and swallowed more carefully. I could see each of us beginning to anticipate what others needed as we passed the salt and pepper without asking, moved chairs and made room for each other to sit down. We learned how much warmth we could convey with our eyes alone; fully 80 per cent of our everyday communication truly is non-verbal. I ate more slowly. I tuned into my body sensations better than I usually do, and when I felt full, I stopped eating. This was an unexpected gift discovered in silence.

I also noticed that my mind flitted from thought to thought like a hummingbird bouncing from flower to flower. I was grateful that our elder guides encouraged us to set an intention for the weekend so we would make the best use of our time. My intention for the weekend was to create a clear, concrete vision for this completed book.

Inspired by Lynda's cross-country odyssey, I'd taken two days to drive from Vancouver Island to Los Gatos, wanting time alone to move gently into this new learning experience. When I was ready to leave after the retreat, I was wide awake at 3:00 a.m., raring to beat as much of San Francisco's early morning rush-hour traffic as possible by hitting the road.

Silence hung in the massive trees, apart from the hollow hooting of a night owl, and all around me was pitch black. Pensively I left my weekend cottage nestled in the woods at the bottom of a steep, crooked little path. My flashlight lit the way as I hauled my luggage, notes and nibbles up at least thirty chipped concrete steps. Two trips up and down, and I was set to go. I laid out my nutritional companions on the seat beside me: power bars, chocolate bars, raisins, almonds, cashews, cheese and water bottles. My headlights illuminated the narrow mountain backcountry road as I hugged its hilly, well-treed, right-hand side, thankful that the sheer drop-off was on the left. I met only one other car carefully making its way down to the highway, and I was grateful to reach the valley floor and pull onto the main road.

A few hours later, with the Los Gatos hills now well behind me, I felt myself expand along with the wide-open, flat landscape surrounding Sacramento. The sun was beginning to peek over the distant horizon as I peacefully continued my drive into the light. I made the first half of the journey in silence and solitude, still cocooned in the quiet energy of the weekend. The miles flew by, and I was barely aware of the landscape as I hummed along the well-kept ribbon of I-5. I made excellent time, and twelve hours later slowly threaded Portland's congested traffic. It was only 3:00 p.m., much too early to stop for the night, so I decided to go the distance. I pulled into one of the many well-kept rest stops, cleaned out the chocolate bar wrappers, changed my now chocolate-stained yellow top, poured myself a cup of tea and brought out a few CDs. Carol Burnett and Stuart McLean kept me wide awake and laughing the rest of the way.

Seventeen hours after leaving Northern California, I crossed the Canadian border, and about twenty-five minutes later I pulled into the lineup at the Tsawwassen ferry terminal south of Vancouver. I called to let Lou know I'd be on the 10:45 p.m. ferry and home shortly after 1:00 a.m. He was stunned. It did indeed feel like quite an accomplishment. I was tired, but on another level also felt as though I'd driven the entire journey in a wide-awake, alert trance. Twenty-four hours in silence had given me a powerful energy surge.

I was glad that I'd taken time to drive to and from Los Gatos. Both journeys allowed for a smooth transition into and out of silence. Both provided ample opportunity for reflection, and my thoughtful hours spent driving home aided me in integrating the gifts the retreat had given me. The long drive, for me at least, was more graceful than flying. However quick and efficient it may be, air travel includes the jarring, unsettling hubbub of most overcrowded airport terminals. We regularly sacrifice quality of experience for speed and efficiency, but I fear we lose untold gems in the process.

Our world is noisy. Unnecessary sound pummels our ears like hailstones on a car roof. Noise, like caffeine, is occasionally delicious but can be addictive and hard to digest. It's best in small, measured doses. Whenever we can slip into silence, away from noise even for a moment, we increase our ability to respond to any situation in a calmer, more reasoned manner. This can take some getting used to. I believe we can all reap real benefit now and again from time in silence. Like anything worthwhile, it gets richer and more profound with practice.

Our collective desire for more moments of silence is definitely increasing. I called a major technical firm this morning, listened to the menu, pushed the buttons and heard the usual message about how important my call was to the company and how all representatives were currently serving other customers; the wait would be about two minutes. Here's the kicker: the disembodied voice added, "If you prefer to wait in silence without music, press the pound key." I pressed the pound key and got silence. If I'd been standing, I would have done a little jig and shouted, "Hallelujah!"

Silence Is My Homeland. The words jumped out at me from a bookshelf in a small gift shop housed in a quaint, sun-bleached cabin at Squirrel Cove on Cortez Island, British Columbia. Lou and I were cruising the waters of the upper Strait of Georgia on our thirty-three-foot sailboat, *Oriental Dawn.* We powered ashore in our patched, faded-blue dinghy to pick up groceries. Finding the book by Gilean Douglas was an unexpected bonus.

The black-and-white sketch on the cover shows a small cabin with four small windows, a peaked roof and two chimney stacks, dwarfed by tall fir trees that are themselves dwarfed by the mountain rising in the background. Snowbanks rise on both sides of the cabin, giving the impression that it is well snuggled in for a cold winter. The cabin looks—depending on one's perspective—either bleak and lonely or warm and inviting. For author Gilean Douglas it was her solitary, silent sanctuary; the surrounding woods were her teacher, companion and provider of abundance for ten years as she carved out for herself a home on the Teal River in the British Columbia wilderness.

Henry David Thoreau also loved the wordless, solitary world of nature and highly recommended it. He believed that returning to a simpler life closer to nature offered an antidote to the "lives of quiet desperation" led by many of his contemporaries. No doubt he would offer similar advice today. Both memoirs, Thoreau's and Douglas's, immediately immerse a reader in the beauty of nature and silence. Word by word and line by line, their writing is an invitation to all of us to spend more time in that world.

My walks are sometimes so silent that I can hear the smooth sound of nylon on nylon as I swing my arms in my lightweight red jacket. This morning I could hear my miniature poodle Yoda's little paws patting the pavement as he trucked along. His companion, Prince, weighs only fourteen pounds and is so light on his feet that he makes no sound at all unless another dog approaches; then his deep-throated growl sounds quite funny coming out of such a little dog. I lifted my eyes as a great blue heron made his way from ocean to distant tree. In silence all our senses wake and become more acute, giving our world and our lives more colour and texture. We come alive in silence.

4

Hidden treasure

ONE WARM FALL DAY WHEN I was ten and had just started grade six, I chanced upon a meditation garden. I didn't know what it was then, but I know now. More than fifty years passed before I thought of it again. It was as though that precious memory, as perfect as the experience, had waited patiently for my invitation to spill its treasure.

Walking home from my school in Southwest Calgary, I felt light-hearted. I preferred walking two and a half miles home from school to sitting on a lumbering city bus and watching the world fly by in a blur. I loved my freedom on foot and delighted in daily adventures. My route that day wound up a hill past stately old mansions set well back from the road and fronted by large manicured lawns. One ivy-covered house stood within a tall hedge at least four feet thick. Had I not been slowly meandering by, I would never have discovered the slight gap between tightly packed branches. It was simply too intriguing to ignore! In I wiggled, leaving behind the daylight and stepping into shadow.

I stopped, looked and listened.

My eyes quickly adjusted to the diffuse light, almost like twilight, filtered by an overhead canopy of thickly intertwined tree branches silhouetted against the sky. The forest floor was free of all debris; I saw not a needle or leaf, as though tender, loving hands had purposely swept clean the dirt. I stood on the lip of a gently rolling slope that drew me farther into the hushed silence. If another child had been with me, we would have held our index fingers to our lips and murmured, Shhh!

Curiosity carried me cautiously forward. I followed a crooked gully down to my right, inching ever deeper into the dark woods. There at the bottom of the incline, hidden from all passing eyes, waited a small bench, a little pagoda and a bridge. I stared and breathed in the peaceful setting, like nothing I had seen before.

The stone bench was all graceful curves along its low back, around its sides and down its four legs. It was just long enough for two children sitting side by side or one adult. The grey concrete pagoda perched on bowed legs at the foot of a tree across from the bench, and a small, curved wooden bridge spanned the narrow gully. The peace and quiet enveloped me and held me spellbound. I don't know how long I stood there before slowly backing away. I wasn't scared—far from it; I felt completely safe—but I knew with a child's sense that I had stumbled uninvited into someone's sacred space.

I was drawn to the garden two more times. Once it was rather like pinching myself to be sure something so magical and mysterious really did exist. The other time I reluctantly said goodbye. I climbed onto the bench and caressed the smooth curve along its back while swinging my feet inches above the ground. I tiptoed across the little bridge and touched the rough top of the pagoda as I passed by. I have a feeling someone else was in the garden that last time, and I like to think that whoever it was could see that I approached with respect and reverence and allowed me to stay. I would dearly love to have returned and met the guardian of the garden.

But duty called. My adventurous explorations, which so suited my nature, also caused me to shirk responsibilities such as picking up my little sister from her school and beginning dinner preparations. I had to get on the bus, leave behind the otherworld magic and move on into the reality of my life, which was anything but quiet or serene. It warms my heart now to speculate that this accidental exposure to silent, simple beauty sowed a seed that in my middle age slowly pulled me toward the tranquility in regular solitude, silence and meditation. All of these feel friendly and familiar.

Meditation is inclusive, an uncomplicated practice in which we can all take part and benefit. We can all create sacred space where we cultivate concentration and rest mind, body and spirit. My meditation practice is simpler now than when I started over twenty-five years ago; I no longer strive to get it right or follow a particular path. For example, I got up this morning while the house was dark, cool and quiet. I put on warm socks, slipped my feet into my favourite sandals, pulled on a pair of baggy blue pants and a sloppy turquoise top and added my old yellow chenille housecoat. Half asleep, I walked softly down the hallway and downstairs to my sanctuary with Yoda padding along behind me. Yoda curled up on his cushy grey bed in the corner of my office while I settled into my high-backed, black upholstered chair, feet resting easily on the floor.

Throughout the night, forty- to fifty-mile-an-hour southeasterly winds and pounding rain had buffeted our house. I could hear the wind in the eighty-foot cedar and fir trees that stand just across the driveway outside my office window. The roar of the wind came and went like wild surf pounding and receding on a beach; an occasional blast sounded as if wind and waves were crashing onto ragged rocks.

I settled in to meditate at 6:30 a.m., fighting a fierce caffeine-withdrawal headache; I was entering day two once again, giving up my rich, delicious mochas, which interfere with my digestion and sleep. I began as usual by resting my hands on my lap, attempting to bring my attention to my breath. But this morning the sound of wind and pummelling rain blasted my quiet office. Nature's sound effects matched the rhythm of my pulsating head, so I breathed gently in and out, listening to the wind in the trees and the rain on the window. My body began to relax, and within fifteen minutes the throbbing had eased to a dull ache like a prickly pressure cap on the top of my head. Another ten minutes of sitting quietly, breathing slowly and reining in my thoughts, and my headache was no longer front and centre. Its pulsating slowed and stopped as the wind and rain eased. At the end of fifty minutes, the storm had passed its prime, and only tendrils of my headache remained. I recorded the process in my journal and then stepped out into the day, smiling. Meditation revitalizes me. It is a perfect way to begin and end each day.

Once I tried to meditate in a group by attending a two-day Zen meditation retreat with about eighty experienced Zen practitioners—all dressed in black shirts and slacks—and a few other newcomers. We sat in a large room with concrete walls and hardwood floors in the Asian Centre at the University of British Columbia. The small patch of grey wall I faced was full of tiny burst air bubbles in the rough concrete; I focused my attention on the tiny, perfect heart they formed. When I close my eyes, I can see it still. I tried hard to fit in and do everything right, but that didn't last long. After our sitting meditation, we did walking meditation. I'd never done it before, and we received no instruction; there seemed to be an expectation that we would follow the person in front and fall into line. At the time I had foot problems that precluded walking without shoes for any distance, but shoes were not permitted in the zendo. Not far into the walking meditation in my stocking feet, I was in considerable pain. I stepped out of the line, bowed properly at the door and quietly left the zendo. Others who had opted out of walking meditation from the start were sitting in the garden foyer, so I joined them. No one spoke.

Later, when we all gathered in the zendo, the teacher announced that stepping out of line during walking meditation was not permitted. I felt embarrassed and angry, like a publicly chastised child. I was also surprised and disappointed at the way the leader had addressed my small transgression. One of the senior members could have taken me aside quietly and explained the protocol.

Tai chi, meditation in motion, is the preferred practice of my friend and tai chi instructor, Bill Perison. A mutual friend of ours once did tai chi with Bill on the hard, sandy beach below Dallas Road in Victoria, British Columbia. When they had finished, Ahmad had thoroughly scuffed the sand, but Bill's movements had barely disturbed it. Bill stands six feet tall, but his movements are light-footed and fluid. They weren't always.

Bill first explored meditation twenty-five years ago as an antidote to the almost paralyzing anxiety he experienced as a young university student in Toronto. At one time, Bill told me, he held himself with such rigidity that his curled toes protruded from the top of his runners. Today, as he enters his fifties, his unlined face, easygoing manner and fluid movements belie his earlier anxiety.

Bill studied for ten years with a Vipassana (or Insight) meditation teacher in Toronto. He attended weekly sitting meditation sessions—students sat on the floor in full lotus position for about an hour—followed by discussions and teachings. He was intimately involved with a meditation community that he loved. Four times a year he practised in a retreat weekend that alternated hours of sitting meditation with either qigong or tai chi.

At two long retreats, one for two weeks and one for a month, he sat for ten hours a day with breaks for meals. Bill still remembers his physical pain during the long, arduous sittings. He most enjoyed chanting and tai chi. Over the years he moved away from any rigid routine or protocol. As I did, he developed his own flexible, fulfilling practice. He much prefers to focus his attention on matching his breath with the demanding movements of tai chi, which he generously and patiently shares with his students.

Calming the mind and paying attention are the essence of meditation, whether sitting, walking or moving with tai chi. We do not have to think thoughts that cause us grief and anxiety. Sometimes it's important to rein in our thoughts, and at other times it's equally important to let them run free. Journal writing is the place to give our thoughts free rein and capture their creative wonder. It's also the supreme place to write out and work through deeply painful personal experiences.

All the stories in this book began in my journal; directly, indirectly, immediately or at some remove they originated in meditation. When I sit down to meditate, I always have journal and pen handy. As soon as I close my eyes and begin to relax, valuable ideas surface that I want to capture; after meditation, a few minutes to write in my journal are essential. My journal is not meant to be shared. Another person has read it only once and without my consent.

When I was a child, not yet a teen, I wrote in my diary about running through the fields and about catching frogs and bumblebees and butterflies. I wrote about real and imaginary adventures and I wrote about my dreams. I also wrote about what I thought and what made me sad. One day my mother read what I wrote. I felt horrified and humiliated in equal measure, and I felt exposed and misunderstood.

In my mid-thirties I returned to personal writing through the impersonal portal of academic writing. One particular course on children and grief required us to tap into our own experience of grief and loss. The floodgates opened. I wrote out twenty years' worth of pent-up emotion before I could pull back sufficiently to write an objective academic paper. But what a treasure that process unveiled! From that day forth I have kept a journal. I write by hand, my head down over the page, cocooned in my own thoughts; it's an entirely different experience than sitting, head and body erect, typing into a computer. I write what I think and feel, including the full range of emotions: pain, anger, frustration, grief, joy and celebration. During the process I inevitably name names, sometimes call names and other times bless people by name.

As I mentioned in Chapter 1, I shredded ten years' worth of journals in one fell swoop in September 2007. But I read before I shredded, and ever since, I have been more conscientious about regularly shredding and burning. If I get hit by a car tomorrow, I do not want to leave an unintended legacy of hurt to my loved ones. Burning or shredding our journals offers an opportunity to let go of the past and move on. It's the process of personal writing—as our thoughts move out of our heads, through our hearts and onto paper—that heals and transforms us. There's no need to retain the paper.

My favourite journals are spiral-bound and 8½ x 11 inches; anything smaller cramps my style because my handwriting is messy. I like the feel of creamy, smooth paper best, but haven't found it locally in the size and binding I prefer, so I settle for standard wide-ruled white paper. I cover about 120 pages a month and always begin a new journal on January 1. Since my journal contains my current feelings about all the happenings in and around my life, it stays in my writing sanctuary.

Meditation and journal writing clear cobwebs from my mind. They improve my memory and concentration, and I believe they help me be more patient and kind. Meditation calms my mind, body and spirit; journal writing gives colour, clarity and vibrancy to my thoughts. Both sustain me. I came to meditation out of curiosity and stayed because of the benefits. I came to diary or journal writing naturally as a child, as most children do, and my mother's reading of my diary robbed me of a precious private outlet. We all need a safe place for our raw emotions and unformed thoughts. The meditation garden of my childhood is long lost, but with journal and pen in hand, I can always revisit the peaceful world of meditation.

Part II

Navigating Rough Waters

5

THE BACKPACK

WHEN I WAS A LITTLE girl, we had a black-and-white dog named Tip for the streak of silver that ran down the middle of her nose and the patch of white that gave character to her tail. At the time we lived in a three-bedroom, green stucco bungalow with wide windows looking out over the grassy backyard. Our yard, backing on to a narrow alley, was bordered on one side by a dilapidated, brown, single-car garage and on the other side by flower beds, my father's delight.

One warm summer day, as I passed the window, I noticed dirt flying from Tip's paws as she happily dug another tunnel around the base of my dad's prized peonies. Dad arrived before I could clean up the mess and hide the hole. Shortly afterward Tip went to live on a farm.

I don't remember how I felt at the time. Certainly I never knowingly grieved; this was probably one of the many items that just went into my "backpack." I forgot about Tip until my younger sister, Liz, reminded me a few years ago. I do know that I've had dogs all my adult life and currently have two. Liz and my older brother, Ferg, also each have two dogs. I never consciously considered Tip when I got my first dog as an adult, but it makes sense to me that this early childhood loss influenced the dog decisions my siblings and I later made.

We are constantly—consciously and unconsciously—completing unfinished business and healing old wounds. It helps us to know and understand the cause of our current passions and proclivities. A little digging will relatively easily uncover this knowledge and understanding.

Life Goes On: Losing, letting go and living again—my first book, recently republished—contains anecdotes, exercises and suggestions to offer readers practical information about how to navigate current and past grief. This subject is dear to my heart because I've found that unresolved grief causes a great deal of emotional, physical and soul pain. It may last a lifetime, robbing us of the good things in life such as pleasure, joy, wonder and gratitude. Our adventures over sixty will most certainly include grief and loss.

Readers have told me that they found some suggestions in *Life Goes On* especially helpful. Grieving is a gentle, practical skill that we all can learn. Four simple steps can help us through every loss we encounter in life: 1) identify the loss, 2) acknowledge and allow the pain, 3) create a ceremony to say goodbye and 4) go forward. This elegant framework, applied with care and attention, will enhance and clarify any grieving process.

The backpack analogy, my clients say, is particularly valuable. Think of it this way: When we're born, we're given a backpack into which we stuff all the painful and confusing experiences of childhood, adolescence and adulthood, including all our losses. Over the years we may, on occasion, choose to take off the backpack and look at the contents, but then again we may not, or we may unload a few and repack the rest. As the years go by, we may upgrade to a bigger pack, quickly close the flap, hoist it onto our shoulders and trudge on; although the burden may weigh us down, it has also become familiar. It may take a current crisis to trigger the pain and grief associated with an earlier loss. If that happens, it's an invitation to explore and unload our backpack of items—large and small—from our past.

Let us not underestimate the power of seemingly small surface losses to unleash deep grief. Loss occurs in contexts that involve other people, places and events; it doesn't occur in isolation. Frequently we need to sift through the circumstances surrounding a previous experience to find their illuminating gold. A single incident may spark multiple losses. Only when we take an item out of our backpack and carefully examine it do we fully understand its true symbolic value.

In September of grade nine, I was sent away to boarding school in Saskatoon, Saskatchewan, far from my friends who didn't meet my mother's approval. Boarding school was a painful disaster; I felt achingly lonely. But I have one marvellous memory from that time. In October, when I came home that first Thanksgiving weekend, my friends threw me a surprise party. I was completely overwhelmed, almost speechless. My friends Shirley, Joyce, Susan and Cheryl decorated Shirley's rumpus room with balloons and colourful crepe paper, but the most magnificent decoration was a wide, shiny, green-and-gold banner that I saw strung across the wall when I walked in. It said, in big bold letters, Welcome Home, Gail.

I squirrelled that banner away in a special cream-coloured box that I placed in a dresser drawer underneath my sweaters. This was a treasure I didn't want to lose. Occasionally throughout my turbulent teens, I would take the banner out, run my hands over the shiny letters, smooth out any crinkles and place the letters lovingly back in their hiding place. They warmed my heart; they meant so much to me. I probably never adequately expressed my gratitude, but I've never forgotten my friends' kindness.

I never saw any of those friends again. I came home only for holidays, and as teens do, we went our separate ways. I was no longer a part of their lives, and they were no longer a part of mine. I didn't make close female friends again until I was well into my thirties. When I was eighteen, my family moved to Victoria. Once we unpacked, I frantically looked for my box of treasures. But they were gone, and this reduced me to tears. It wasn't losing the letters themselves that caused my grief but what they symbolized: firm friendship, youth, the city in which I grew up and more. Symbolic loss can indeed cause grief.

Understanding what a loss symbolizes is crucial to understanding the power of the past to cause such deep pain today. It's not the magnitude of the loss that's most important but what it represents. A healthy curiosity, an open mind and a willingness to revisit the experience will provide rich information and clear direction on what and how to grieve. Purposeful grieving helps us say a friendly hello to the past, wave a healthy goodbye and more warmly welcome the future.

As we move into our senior years, we naturally want to lighten our load, though not many people need to produce five bags of confetti as I did when I began this journey. It may come as a surprise that unloading our backpack needn't take long or be difficult. For every painful memory that requires a closer look, we'll discover at least two or three that cause us no more pain.

Our restless pain is more like a weed than an inert rock. Weeds reach for the sun; they keep pushing for the light. All we need to do is show up, open the backpack and begin sorting. Whatever wants to see the light of day will rise to the surface. Some memories will make us laugh, others will make us cry and many will do both; some will be gentle and life-affirming, and others still may startle us with strong emotions. All help us complete our quest and come home to ourselves, knowing fully who we are and what now matters most.

Triggers also proved to be a valuable concept for many readers of *Life Goes On*. In the context of a grieving process, a trigger is any current event that produces an unexpectedly strong emotional response—a response that seems out of proportion in the immediate situation. We all have different triggers. Songs and smells can evoke both pleasant and unpleasant memories.

A trigger alerts us that another item in our backpack needs attention.

Voice can be a violent trigger, particularly the voice of authority, if that authority was used to intimidate and abuse. The voice could belong to a former teacher or supervisor, an abusive old flame or a long-absent parent who suddenly reappears on the scene. When we're caught off guard or blindsided, we get thrown back emotionally into feeling like a vulnerable child facing a bully. This can happen to us at any age, and it helps to gently ask ourselves how old we feel in the moment. The answer will provide invaluable information and direction. One thing is for sure: if we feel like we're five, even if we're fifty-five, it will take some work to regain our equilibrium.

My former client James calls infrequently, perhaps only once or twice a year, and only when his abusive mother has visited. Even though he's now fifty-four, she can quickly reduce him to a quivering child. James has done a good deal of effective grief work, so he well knows and understands the cause of his shaky legs. Feelings of inadequacy now only flood him momentarily, and he can quickly withdraw and get grounded with a vigorous walk and firm resolve. His feelings are completely understandable, given his history, yet he does find these moments frustrating and disconcerting.

Triggers are powerful. They can affect us when we attend a friend's celebration of life, watch a movie, read a novel, hear an ambulance or see flashing lights. If we find ourselves sobbing at the funeral of someone we hardly knew, we may want to question whether our sorrow is actually for someone closer to us who died within the last few years or perhaps even in our childhood. Asking, Who am I crying for? may shed some light on whom and what we need to grieve. Knowing and understanding the true cause of our tears can be reassuring. Special occasions and anniversaries of a loved one's death, even many years later, frequently trigger painful emotion. If you find yourself particularly restless, agitated or sleepless as you read this chapter, asking yourself what these feelings remind you of may help you uncover the cause.

We need to trust the answers that bubble up from our unconscious and work with them by writing in our journal, talking to a friend or perhaps making a collage of the memory. Invite it in, and it will lose its sting. If we give grief our attention and watch it dissipate, it will hold us back no more. When a memory no longer evokes a strong emotional response and we can talk about it without our voice cracking, we know our grief work is complete. We can't think our way through grief, which is inherently emotional. Once we apply the four steps of a healthy grieving process to losses large and small, we may find that life looks brighter and our backpack weighs much less.

Each of us is a work in progress, like an intricate, colourful jigsaw puzzle. When a piece of the puzzle falls into place, we feel comforted and affirmed. It is an aha! moment. Our life picture is more complete. As seniors we see ourselves and our lives through a more multi-faceted lens now than we did in our youth or middle age. We can draw on our greater body of information, experience, personal strength, skill and resources. We may also have more time and incentive to clear the decks and start anew. In our senior years, healthy grieving is a trustworthy path to serenity.

6

LETTING GO

M Y FRIEND MICKEY CALLED ME recently in tears. She was doing a spring cleaning in the fall, going through old papers and binders, crying all the while. Purging, she called it, weeping for "the loss of my job, my career, my identify, my self-esteem and my passion." I called it grieving.

I've known Mickey for more than thirty years; when I taught effective parenting classes in the early eighties, she was one of my first students. We became friends out of mutual respect and a desire to help others. Mickey dedicated her life to rescuing lost adolescents; for twenty years she worked for a local family service organization that she loved with all her heart. She loved her employers, supervisors and colleagues; she also loved her clients, who were confused, lonely and utterly lost teens. She willingly gave hard work and loyalty far beyond her job's requirements.

When the organization lost lucrative contracts, forcing it to close programs, it dismissed Mickey and other experienced long-time staffers. Mickey continued to promote the organization—working with management, creating new programs and raising funds—until it went through a rebirth about eighteen months later. Mickey expected to get her job back, but it became clear that new management was willing to sacrifice street-smart senior childcare workers for recent university graduates. Loyalty, experience, considerable skill, talent and passion counted for naught. At fifty-eight Mickey was out in the cold, and it brought her to her knees.

Mickey had coped with loss before and knew the value of saying goodbye in order to move on. An actual ceremony—involving body, mind and heart—would work best. Her purging, grieving and saying goodbye to the past meant reviewing her excellent performance evaluations, accolades heaped on her from her organization, her gold-plated reference letters, hand-written notes from grateful parents and teens, some of them former street kids whom Mickey had literally picked up off the street and cajoled, loved and guided back onto a healthy path.

As she absorbed the love these letters contained, I watched her come alive. The letters reminded her of her enormous gifts and her worthwhile contribution to many lives. She had made a difference! Their gratitude now helped her heal and pull herself out of the depths. She unloaded old, unhappy baggage, let go of the past and the pain and turned her love of life to other pursuits. She worked hard to regain her composure and her passion, and though it took her well over a year to land a new job, she never gave up.

Mickey now works part-time as an education assistant with special-needs children. She still receives excellent performance evaluations because she values her colleagues and supervisors, and above all, loves the children she works with. And they love her. Mickey also makes massive hanging baskets for the plant nursery she owns with her husband. Her beautiful blooming baskets—always containing colourful spring surprises—are in increasing demand. She now also runs a gift shop full of quirky, original items. Her door is always open.

One cool December morning at 8:00 a.m. we met briefly for coffee; Mickey likes to arrive at work early, prepare and be fully present for the young children she'll work with that day. She had a small gift for me, a new hand cream that she'd discovered would smooth and heal her chapped hands, and she was giving tubes to friends for Christmas. I was thrilled to see her once again with a glowing face, vibrant and alive.

We can all mine our experiences, as Mickey did, for the gifts they contain. Waste nothing! We can transform our pain and sorrow into gratitude, compassion and love of life. This is the essence of letting go. Done compassionately and consciously, the grieving process provides an antidote to depression.

People today acknowledge depression more readily than sadness; somehow it has become more socially acceptable. When friends, colleagues or clients tell me they're depressed, I ask how they're acting or feeling differently. Invariably they say they're sad, maybe weepy, feeling stuck, lacking initiative, low in energy, unfocused or unable to concentrate. All these are symptoms of grief. Then I wonder out loud what is now happening in their lives and what that might represent. As they talk and I listen, I usually see understanding dawn on their face. How they feel begins to make sense. They feel better and more grounded.

Not all grief is old or unresolved, of course; much is current but unidentified. Once we identify it, we can resolve it.

Recently a woman called to inquire about my coaching services. As is common on a first, tentative phone call, she wasn't particularly forthcoming, but she did say she felt unsettled and maybe a bit depressed. I didn't press for details, since we hadn't established a working relationship, but I answered her questions and told her of my specialty in grief and loss. My caller said she had no grief issues, but in the next breath, told me she would retire soon.

Retirement is a minefield of grief and loss issues, specific and symbolic, as is any major life transition. Some resistance to change is innate. Even when we're happily anticipating a well-deserved retirement, it's worthwhile to honestly consider what we are giving up as well as what we'll gain. When we retire, at the very least we're letting go of our career and some collegial camaraderie. Failure to acknowledge the myriad losses associated with retirement seems to me a bit lopsided. I would opt for a more balanced approach that includes integration of losses and gains, which is more likely to ensure a fun-filled future.

Reframing depression as possibly unidentified—and therefore unresolved—grief gives us an action plan and a healthy focus to help us get unstuck. The grieving process is holistic, encouraging self-knowledge and integration. Our priorities begin to crystallize, and we're more able to set realistic goals. Grieving soothes guilt, eases anger and rage, reduces or eliminates regret and promotes forgiveness. Sadness evaporates. The lines of our face soften, and a sparkle returns to our eyes. The entire process is life-enhancing.

Letting go can be a challenge. For some of us it feels like freefall after being pushed out of a fast-moving airplane. We tumble around for a while before we remember to pull the rip cord on our parachute and drift safely to the ground. How we land depends on our earlier planning and experience.

So it is with the grieving process. When we plunge into grief, at first it's difficult to get our bearings, and for a long time we may truly not know which way is up or down. Following the steps of a healthy grieving process offers a rip cord; it will orient you correctly and deposit you standing firmly on your feet, as it did Mickey. Effective grieving is the perfect parachute.

7
DIMMING LIGHTS

MY MOTHER'S LIGHT DIMMED AND went out just before sunrise on Valentine's Day 1981. I was with her for the twelve hours before she died. The nursing sister brought us tea and cookies in the early evening, straightened Mum's pillows and stopped in periodically throughout the night. Mum was mentally alert, physically exhausted, and emotionally drained when she died too young at sixty-two.

Mum's end in a small, private room was peaceful, but her lengthy dying process was not. She died of emphysema—now called chronic obstructive pulmonary disease—complicated by osteoporosis caused by the steroid drugs prescribed to relieve her breathing. She was on oxygen full-time for the two years before her death. In the end even laughter caused her pain.

In her final two years of life, with considerable heartache, we moved her from her unusual five-sided house on a hill to a small, gracious retirement facility by the sea and finally into a large, unfeeling, acute care hospital. There she languished until a bed became available at a nursing home in downtown Victoria. A few years ago it was demolished and rebuilt a short distance away; the lovely new building is all glass, light and beauty. But that came too late for my dear mother.

Mum chose to spend her last three months of life in a nursing home of her choice, turning down invitations to live with my family or with my brother and his wife, Joy, a nurse. Tragically, fiercely independent to the end, she remained lonely and walled off from the love and care her children would have provided. She was a product of her upbringing, her time and her culture, and she knew no other way. She never discussed the fact that she was dying with any family member. It simply wasn't done.

I didn't realize it then, but I now believe Mum knew she was dying. Aside from feeling more comfortable with medical professionals—particularly the three aging Roman Catholic nursing sisters at the facility she chose—she probably also wanted to shield us from her dying process. Her misplaced need to protect us did not serve any of us well.

The four-storey nursing home in downtown Victoria was bleak, smelly, old, cold, noisy and thoroughly depressing. It broke my heart to take her there. Even thirty years later, the day I moved her stands out as one of the worst days of my life. I don't think Mum really noticed her surroundings; she was just too tired and too ill. She was far more ready to go than I was to let her go. But I didn't understand that then and I felt powerless to make anything any better. Writing about it all these years later still brings tears to my eyes and makes my throat seize. I'm not alone in my anguish; with varying degrees of guilt and grief, similar scenarios play out daily in many countries around the world.

Six years later, when I was completing my graduate degree in counselling psychology, I had the opportunity to work and study in a hospital-based hospice for a year. What a breath of fresh air! It was a wonderfully different way of caring for the terminally ill. I did research for my graduate thesis and worked with dying patients and their family members. I was blessed with the wisest, most patient clinical supervisor I've ever had the privilege to work with. In both theory and practice, Emma—a gifted, gentle mentor—introduced me to gratitude.

My first hospice patient, Maria, was dying of amyotrophic lateral sclerosis or Lou Gehrig's disease. ALS is a cruel disease. Death is not normally quick; muscle atrophy and nerve degeneration usually proceed slowly for up to five years. Mental ability is not affected, so people know what's happening to them as they gradually become trapped in their bodies.

Emma took me into Maria's room to introduce me. Soft music played in the background from a small bedside radio, and muted sunshine came in through the open window. All the staff maintained relaxing music for Maria. She lay in bed, unable to move her wasted legs or muscle-atrophied arms. Her hair lay limp on the pillow, but she greeted us with bright eyes. Her throat muscles were now affected, and though she could still hear, she could no longer speak. She communicated with blinks and facial expressions.

Before being struck down by ALS, I believe, Maria taught music. Shortly after we met, she was taken on her last excursion to hear a local concert. I was in her room when she returned. Joy accompanied her, born of gratitude. I could feel her gratitude for the experience and see it in her eyes. She beamed. I asked Emma, "How can she feel so grateful?" That was just Maria's way, Emma said. She truly was grateful for all the care and kindness she received. Before she lost the ability to speak, she'd thanked people verbally. Now she could only express her gratitude with her eyes.

Gratitude was common at the hospice. In spite of suffering and impending death, patients and family endlessly expressed their genuine gratitude for all the care. Maria was dying painfully and slowly but with as much dignity and gratitude as she could muster. She still found moments of joy.

Permit me to honour a friend by describing another dying process. Bev Abbey was a welcoming, generous colleague who was an indefatigable promoter for her favourite causes. She had a way of cajoling and encouraging active participation in our professional association as its successful, consensus-building president. I admired Bev's integrity and still miss our frequent energetic discussions. When she and her husband, Bob Drummond, returned from their yearly three-month holiday to Mazatlan, Mexico, in the spring of 2007, she felt unwell. Once all the medical results were in, the news was devastating.

Bev deteriorated quickly over the next few months and died of cancer on November 29, 2007.

Bev spent some time in an acute care hospital and later a hospice, but she spent the last few days of her life at home, where she died surrounded by her large, loving family. She made time to say goodbye to friends, family members and colleagues who visited during her final weeks. Her son, my friend Darin Abbey, a compassionate registered nurse, became her gatekeeper to protect her waning energy and her time. When I was unable to get to Vancouver, Bev asked Darin to call me to say how much she esteemed our collegial relationship. I was deeply touched. Darin and I periodically talked on the phone until the evening before Bev died. Her life was a shining example of compassion for all; even while dying she remained thoughtful and considerate.

Medical needs can be so complex in some situations that dying at home isn't an option. There is no absolutely right course of action; these difficult decisions call for thought and open family discussion. It's never far from my mind that I'm just a few years older than my mother was when she died. My painful experience fuels and informs my ongoing discussions with my husband, sons, siblings, friends, doctor and lawyer. The more we discuss these things while we're vibrantly alive, the better.

Except in cases of sudden death, we can do much to influence how and where we die if we discuss this before it's too late. How we approach this delicate subject depends on our cultural and religious background, our personal experiences of death and our resulting beliefs and philosophies. The older we are, the more we've been touched by death.

All our lights will eventually dim and go out. Maria, my mother and Bev each died differently: Maria would have had ample opportunity to discuss any fears or concerns in the hospice's comfortable, supportive environment; Bev was always one to confront difficult subjects, and I'm sure she brought this approach to her death; my mother never spoke of dying.

At the time I lacked the knowledge and skill to open the conversation with Mum, and although I now have that ability, I also respect that denial has its place. Denial, at least outwardly and with her children, enabled my mother to hold it together. For her that was essential and allowed her to die with dignity. It's crucial that we honour each person's choices, however personally difficult we may find those choices. Kindness and an attitude of "do no harm" must always guide our intentions.

8

DRAWING TOGETHER

A LIGHT CAME ON IN the world when you came into it. When you leave, it will go out, never to be replaced.

Most of us don't think of ourselves as lights in the world. We're more inclined to reserve that thought for others and still more inclined to be concerned about their dying process than our own. It is a difficult thing, death. We've been walking hand in hand with it since birth, but we consign thoughts of our death to the nether regions of our mind. Too much focus on death, we would all agree, is morbid.

I considered leaving any discussion of dying and death out of this book. Why raise an unpopular and frequently unpleasant subject? This book is *Adventures Over Sixty*, after all, and adventures are meant to be exciting and exhilarating. But as new learning experiences, adventures are often also fraught with unforeseen obstacles and unexpected twists in the road that painfully contribute to our hard-won wisdom. The more research we do and the more we discuss plans with our travelling companions before a journey, the more likely we are to respond practically and compassionately to uncomfortable surprises. This reduces unnecessary pain and suffering. Our dying process is a journey. Some of us will face a sudden unexpected ending, but most will have time to prepare.

The Last Lecture by Randy Pausch is inspiring. In September 2006, at forty-six, Randy was diagnosed with cancer. In August 2007, when chemotherapy no longer controlled his growing tumours, he learned he was terminally ill. He died in July 2008. Between diagnosis and death he lived a lifetime, leaving a profound legacy for the world, his wife, Jai, and their three young children. Randy desperately wanted to give The Last Lecture so his children would later be able to really see and appreciate him in his element, lecturing at Carnegie Mellon University.

"I lectured about the joy of life, about how much I appreciated life, even with so little of my own left," he wrote in his book introduction. "I talked about honesty, integrity, gratitude, and other things I hold dear. And I tried very hard not to be boring." He was far from boring; he was funny, wise and loving. The day before his lecture was his wife's birthday. As the highlight of his lecture he had a large cake wheeled onto the stage and asked four hundred people to sing her "Happy Birthday." Randy prepared well for his death and left the world smiling amid the tears at his premature passing.

The first time I witnessed a generous, giving attitude in a dying person was on a training video I watched many years ago at Victoria Hospice. The interviewer asked an elderly cancer patient if she ever questioned, "Why me?" As she lay on her side in bed with her soft eyes fixed on the camera, she replied calmly, "No. I ask, Why not me?"

Cultivating an attitude of giving back and concern for others gives meaning and purpose to the lives of people who are dying and eases their dying process. They and their lives still matter. Neither the woman in hospice nor Randy expressed any self-pity, and both continued to contribute and teach to the end and beyond. Through their interviews, lecture and video they still teach us today. What an inspiring gift!

I have seen what happens both when people avoid discussing death and dying and when they invite open discussion about everything that needs to be considered. The difference is night and day. I have worked in hospital and hospice settings and seen the face of death; with proper care and forethought it is not frightening. We're generally more concerned with how we'll die than death itself; once we address our concerns about lucidity, comfort and pain control, we rest easier.

When there's no discussion, friends and relatives frequently function in isolation. Pretense and protection stalk the room, and tension fills the air; nobody talks honestly about the sad reality that a loved one is slipping away before their eyes. This can go on for months and intensify in the final days. A conspiracy of silence, even from the best intentions, serves no one well, least of all the dying.

When families come together to talk about their pain and confusion, on the other hand, there are naturally tears but also laughter and light-hearted banter. Time becomes a friend, not an enemy. Aunts, uncles, parents, children, friends and siblings may gather to share stories that connect the generations. Funny experiences and poignant memories bubble to the surface, and new ones take shape. Opportunities arise to realize realistic dreams and renew relationship bonds. Deep love may be expressed with warmth and joy right alongside the sadness and sorrow. This special time together becomes a celebration of the dying person's life that continues after their passing. The dying feel cherished and included. The transition is smoother and less painful for all, and loved ones left behind draw together rather than drifting apart in their grief.

A good death defies definition; each of us and our family decide that in the context of our lives. The choice is extremely personal and culturally defined; in some situations the dying and their families will choose acute care, hooked up to all that modern technology can provide. In our culture this is currently the norm. Other patients, including me, will want to be at home without machines or technology. Most of us, however, would choose to be pain-free with good management of symptoms such as nausea, breathing difficulties, restlessness and insomnia.

These days there is no medical reason why we can't control all forms of pain and various symptoms in hospital and often at home. Palliative care nurses often tell dying patients, "we can control your pain, but some pain medication will make you groggy and affect your speech. Some will hasten death. Our goal is to make you as comfortable as possible." The focus of palliative care is comfort, which includes consideration of a patient's desire to be alert and able to interact with family as long as possible. It is a delicate balance that knowledgeable palliative care physicians and nurses can maintain.

Being able to say goodbye to those I love would be a major part of a good death for me; so would ensuring there are no leftover, unresolved hard feelings. But once improvement and survival are no longer options, I would prefer the process to draw to a quick close. I'd like to die in my home, with flowers beside my bed and sunlight streaming in through an open window. Bird song would be a bonus. Above all I would ask for compassionate, patient and kind care. And when I am gone, as I've already told my husband, Lou, and sons, Joey and Marty, I would like to sponsor a bench beside the sea with a bronze plaque that reads, Forever Free to Fly.

9

A GENEROUS GESTURE

CRAIG STRUGGLED VALIANTLY FOR ALMOST twelve months against lung cancer that was now spreading to his brain. Accepting that he wasn't going to get any better, he told his wife, Miranda, that he wanted to hold a goodbye party. He didn't want a wake after he died; he wanted to hear what people would say about him and to thank the many who had helped him along the way. He wanted one last fling before the final curtain came down on his life.

Miranda was at first reluctant, as were their two adult children. But Craig was still forceful, and although it took awhile, they eventually granted him this one last wish. They didn't feel as though they had much time to pull this together, so they enlisted close friends and delegated duties such as securing a hall, organizing a caterer, preparing a video, choosing music, sending out invitations and receiving replies. This celebration of Craig's life would have a twist; he would be there to contribute and to bask in the love of his family, friends and colleagues.

Lou liked and respected his former business colleague, so we readily attended his goodbye party. Craig was a strong natural leader and a gregarious people person who had touched many during his life. His friends stepped up to the mike and regaled us all with powerful, funny stories of Craig's escapades. Distant friends sent telegrams. Craig was pleased with his celebration, as were his wife and children. It gave them an opportunity to see their husband and father through others' eyes.

But Craig didn't die quickly; he lingered for a few months, and some people who had attended his party found this awkward. Perhaps that didn't matter. The love and caring that Craig and his family absorbed at the party carried them all more gently toward his death. That was what mattered to him, as it mattered to those of us who did attend, because we felt as though we'd all contributed in some small way to easing his dying process.

Planning and preparation for our own death is a generous and kind-hearted gesture. It is an opportunity to provide clear direction that can prevent the confusion and controversy that so frequently accompany death and dying. Most of us over sixty have wills, if for no other reason than to spare our family from paying high court fees if we die without one. Nor do we want to leave the dispersal of our precious possessions up to chance or to a court-appointed administrator.

End-of-life medical directives, medical power of attorney and other terms vary in different jurisdictions, but their meaning is the same. This medical and legal document, duly signed and witnessed, appoints someone—usually a spouse, partner, parent, mature adult child or other dependable family member or friend—to make medical decisions for us if we're unable to make our own. It also sets out in detail how each of us defines quality of life and, in the absence of that quality of life, the medical interventions we find acceptable.

My Aunt Joan, my mother's younger sister, lived alone. In the spring of 2006, at eighty-four, she died in Vancouver General Hospital. In the year before her death she was brought to one or another of Vancouver's hospital emergency rooms at least half a dozen times. My brother, Ferg, was with her at St. Paul's the first time she was asked about her end-of-life wishes. This type of discussion was simply not acceptable in Joan's generation of my mother's family, certainly not between an aunt and nephew, however dear and close they were. Ferg was close to Aunt Joan for many years before she died and attended all her emergency hospitalizations.

On one occasion both Joan and my brother were shocked by questions about end-of-life wishes that a young emergency doctor asked abruptly and insensitively. Ferg remembers Joan— seriously ill, fearful and confused—looking at him out of cloudy, liquid eyes with an unspoken question: What on earth is that strange young man asking me? We later learned that emergency room doctors now routinely ask those questions; the preferences we state will give valuable information that can influence essential medical decisions.

When Joan entered Vancouver General for the final time, the emergency doctor was caring and sensitive. After discussion with my brother, he realized the hospital had a substantial file on Joan and knew her wishes from previous admissions. She languished in an emergency room bed for a couple of days before moving to a large, airy room. Three days later my brother and his wife, Joy, sat on either side of her bed holding her hands as she died relatively peacefully.

Any of us at any age could have a serious accident resulting in cognitive impairment. A person can live a long time with diminished capacity. If we're unable to make decisions for ourselves and have no medical directives in place, a public trustee is appointed to act on our behalf. In Canada this legal appointment is intended to protect the interests of children or other vulnerable individuals. If we prefer that a trusted family member make these decisions, it's important to consult a lawyer and have the proper documents prepared.

Openly discussing these sensitive topics with close family members while we're in good health makes it easier for everybody. After signing the papers, we can file them appropriately, raise a toast to the good health of all and continue to live with gusto, knowing we've prepared as well as we possibly can.

Consider how heart-wrenching and difficult it is to discuss these matters with a loved one who is seriously ill. And imagine discussing them for the first time in an emergency room! The thin curtains offer little privacy. If a loved one has diminished cognitive capacity, the situation is well-nigh impossible and can quickly become a medical and legal nightmare. Doctors need to make immediate medical decisions. The medical team will consult with the family, and as long as all members are of one mind, the process may well proceed with compassion and dignity. But families are not always of one mind, and in that case signed, sealed and delivered requests can be inestimably valuable.

My father-in-law Gus's two-year dying process proceeded without legal wrangling largely because the family was of one mind. In 1990, when Gus was eighty-six, a stroke left him speechless and totally paralyzed. The public trustee in the province of Manitoba, where Gus lived, was appointed to oversee his care and administer his estate. The need for a medical power of attorney or directives had never occurred to Gus or any other family member.

Gus was physically short, quiet and hard-working, a man whom others sometimes underestimated. In his younger days he'd been a resourceful, successful and self-reliant prairie farmer. He would have been horrified at a government official making any decisions for him. And although Lou's older brother, Rollie, was named in Gus's will as his executor, he had no such legal standing while their father was still alive; wills come into effect only after we die. It took a painful and costly court process to have Rollie appointed as trustee. Fortunately all family members were in absolute agreement; legal documents flew between the widely dispersed siblings, who quickly signed, notarized and returned them.

For the next two years, until Gus died, Rollie still had to appear regularly in front of a judge to answer questions about how he was caring for his father. Rollie told us about one exchange in particular that made us all shake our heads.

Having seen Rollie several times previously, the judge on Gus's case asked why he hadn't bought his father any shoes.

Rollie, surprised at the insensitive question, could only surmise that the judge had either never read the file or simply wasn't listening. He took a moment to compose himself before answering, "Your honour, my father is paralyzed. He can't walk. He doesn't need shoes."

Part III

Tacking

10

My body, my friend

E very June my cousin Rose leaves the big city of Vancouver and spends three months in her cozy RV at Heriot Bay Campground and Marina on Quadra Island in the upper Strait of Georgia. In the summer of 2010 Lou, my brother, Ferg, his wife, Joy, and I spent five glorious summer days with Rose. Ferg, Joy and their West Highland terrier, Rufus, arrived in their RV. Lou and I brought our miniature poodles, Yoda and Prince, on our sailboat, *Oriental Dawn*, and moored at the marina.

All five of us are seniors. At the time Joy was in considerable pain from a pinched nerve in her back that limited her walking but didn't otherwise dampen her spirits. Lou sprained his foot and hobbled around with the aid of a carved black willow cane that my brother made. Ferg has long suffered knee pain from adolescent football and hockey injuries, now no doubt made worse by age-related osteoarthritis. He is made of stern stuff, however, and rarely lets his aches and pains slow him down.

Rose and I, who both had serious health problems in our twenties, are now passionate advocates of the life-changing benefits of exercise, particularly walking. She happily introduced me to a couple of her favourite Quadra Island hikes. Walking also gave us the opportunity to swap stories. On one of our goat-trail scrambles she told me of a painful but life-changing experience.

"I was in my twenties when I was diagnosed with a common but painful lower back problem, a degenerative disc condition. When I was thirty-three, in 1980, a disc ruptured, leaving me crawling around on all fours much of the time. I had a back operation and the disc was removed.

"After painful rehab, I returned to my favourite sports of skiing, tennis and hiking. Then in 2003, when I was fifty-six, my back went out again, leaving me unable to sit or lie down—or frankly to do just about anything—without pain. The only comfortable position was standing, so I ate my meals at the counter. This went on for several months.

"The back experts said I needed another operation, which I dreaded but would have done, had I not discovered the book *Pain Free* by Pete Egoscue with Roger Gittines. After about six months of following their program, I made progress and ultimately returned to tennis, hiking, kayaking and my two- to three-hour walks. Body health is always a work in progress. I am aware of movement and alignment to help me move in balance, efficiently and pain-free."

Rose credited *Pain Free: A Revolutionary Method for Stopping Chronic Pain* with changing her life. What really changed her life, of course, was that she enthusiastically embraced and applied Egoscue's method. To this day she walks miles, hikes regularly, stretches with yoga and plays a vigorous game of tennis. I picked up Egoscue's book and now use his exercises to relieve any pain as it occurs in my feet, legs, knees, back or neck. The exercises, well set out in the book, are sensible and accessible. And they work.

We are like an intricately woven tapestry; body, mind and spirit together create a complete work of art. We need only look at any newborn baby to realize the wonder that each one of us has evolved from and into. We are given this mobile, ever-changing gift at birth with the freedom to use it as we wish. Few of us receive any instruction in how to care for our bodies with the love, respect and gratitude they deserve. Body care, aside from cosmetic care, didn't figure large for most of us reared in the forties, fifties and sixties.

Since the late seventies, however, a veritable explosion of articles, books, videos and websites have informed us about balanced nutrition, physical fitness, meditation and all activities that reduce stress, awaken latent creative abilities and keep us mentally alert and fully engaged in life. How we move is not half as important as that we move, and the more we move in a variety of different ways the better.

I have no special athletic abilities, and like most of us, I detested school gym classes. I was awkward, uncoordinated and always the last picked to join mandatory softball teams. I started smoking at eleven; that's what the popular girls did, and

I wanted to belong. I still remember a girl named Vina coaching me through my first nauseating drags. Had I quit then, I would very likely have avoided the ill health I was plagued with in my early twenties, including a bout of life-threatening double bacterial pneumonia. My doctor said the Grim Reaper came entirely too close for comfort. Lou and I were just newly engaged, looking forward to getting married in a few months. I was young, with my whole life ahead of me, but the future did not look promising.

I made a major lifestyle change. I quit smoking and began walking and swimming for my life. Book by book, tape by tape and course by course I wheezed, gasped and groaned my way back to health. By trial and error I learned what I needed to know to reverse my unhealthy trend and take charge of my own health. My first exercise class in 1969 was at the Victoria YWCA. I was the youngest in the class by at least thirty years and really felt out of place. But the senior women welcomed me, and every one of them expressed the wish that she had begun to exercise at my age. In the beginning I couldn't keep up with any of them during exercises in the gym or swimming pool. They inspired and encouraged me to continue.

I now wear a pedometer every day and do my best to walk fifteen thousand steps daily, though I'm delighted if I get over ten thousand. As the end of the day approaches, if I haven't yet taken my ten thousand steps, I walk around the yard, in and out of the rooms in the house, up and down the stairs and back around again. Ten thousand steps, I understand, is the magic health maintenance number, and maintaining my vibrant health is my number one priority. Rose and I have a lot of incentive.

My old pedometers needed replacing in the fall of 2010. I contacted Pacific Rim Wellness in Victoria to order two of their CoreHealth pedometers, one for myself and one for Lou. The slogan on the face of the pedometer is "Step up and be a winner." With the pedometers we received information on how to hook up to the CoreLite Virtual Journeys walking program, which allows us to input our steps so that we can virtually walk the Great Wall of China, Circle Canada or Route 66, or go trekking in Nepal—all in the comfort of our own neighbourhood.

When I called Pacific Rim Wellness, the director of operations, Peter Mason, was just heading out for his daily walk in North Saanich, British Columbia. For the last five years he's never missed a day of walking ten thousand steps. Peter proudly told me that his senior sister, Brenda, took up walking after four different doctors told her she would have a stroke or heart attack within two years. Since then she has lost a hundred pounds and regularly places and wins medals in her division in 10 Ks and half-marathons. Peter and his sister are a powerful inspiration.

In 1996 a bone density scan showed that I had osteopenia, the precursor to osteoporosis. Osteoporosis, a dreaded condition of old age, was a major component of my mother's death at sixty-two, but I was only forty-nine. Osteoporosis means brittle, porous bones prone to fracture, particularly in the hip, spine and wrist. The loss of mobility and freedom that would result from a fracture in any one of these areas terrifies me. By

77

1996 I was long committed to an active lifestyle—at the time it included running, cycling and swimming—but though I'd tried three local gyms for varying lengths of time, I finally stopped. I am simply not comfortable in that atmosphere. But I knew that weight training would round out my program and particularly strengthen my wrists, ankles and knees. So I turned, as I usually do, to books.

Strong Women Stay Young, by Miriam E. Nelson, PhD, with Susan Wernick, PhD, caught my eye when it first came out in 1997. It was timely indeed. I was intrigued by the claim that I could reverse bone loss by following an at-home strength-training program in just two sessions a week. I picked up a set of dumbbells—three, five and ten pounds—and ordered a set of ankle weights that I still use. Then I got started.

Research at the Tufts University Centre on Aging with senior men and women from sixty to ninety years found that just two sessions a week, even with the frail elderly, can bring substantial improvement. Dr. Nelson wrote, "If you've lost strength, you can regain it. . . . If you feel older than you like, you can feel younger, stronger and more vigorous—perhaps better than you've ever felt in your entire life." I've been following her program two or three times a week for twenty to thirty minutes on and off for fifteen years and walking almost every day. Bone density scans in 2004 and 2008 showed no evidence of osteopenia or osteoporosis, a true victory to celebrate!

In January 2012, as if to prove to myself that I really do not have brittle bones, I took a nasty fall. Walking with a friend, I stepped from a grassy yard down to the beach by way of a stump. The stump was covered with black ice, and my feet went out from under me. I landed hard on the stump on my tailbone, whacked my neck and head on the concrete wall, landed on my right wrist, got up, shook myself off and continued walking, almost completely unscathed. My head ached for twenty-four hours, the multicoloured black-and-red bruises on my backside took days to fade, and I remained stiff when walking for about five days. My right wrist, at first thought to be broken and immobilized in a cast for six days, showed no discernible fracture on a subsequent X-ray. Within two weeks I was completely healed.

I incorporate appropriate lifting and exercise into my daily routine. Our wood stove heats our house, and I load the wood-box and build many of the fires. When I walk around my yard adding steps to my day, I carry a three-pound weight. I keep one on my desk to lift when I talk on the phone or consider a blank page on my computer. I get up from the computer every twenty to thirty minutes. My inexpensive, comprehensive program of walking, weight training, cycling and stretching exercises has evolved over forty-three years in response to my ever-changing health needs and circumstances. A combination of being outside in nature and daily walking whenever possible never fails to lift both my spirits and my energy.

All of us can do a great deal to ensure we grow old gracefully with a full range of mobility and mental alertness. We'll all grow older, but we don't have to become prematurely marginalized due to ill health. Our own well-being needs to have a high priority. Investment in our health is just as important as any financial plan, if not more so. Good health makes it easier for us to adjust to all circumstances, and it's as close as our next step.

Our bodies are our friends, though most of us have largely ignored them except when they're ailing. When we're seriously ill, many of us say that our bodies have let us down. The truth is that we've let our bodies down. Much illness, disease, disability and chronic pain arises because we've taken our beautiful bodies for granted and not given them the love and attention they require to function at their best. Few of us would expect friends to rush to our assistance if we'd misused, abused and ignored them for lengthy periods of time. The good news is that as soon as we pay attention to our body with beneficial physical activity, like a true friend, it will respond in kind.

Walking greatly enhances my life, and I'm a firm believer in the life-transforming benefits—physical, emotional and spiritual—of movement. The more we move, the more we're able to move and the happier, more alert, more energetic and more flexible we'll become.

Will you walk with me?

11

COURSE CHANGE

THIS MORNING I MADE COFFEE. I measured out the coffee grounds, filled the water reservoir, flipped on the coffee maker and turned away to tend to something else. When I turned back, thick black coffee, full of grounds, was flowing over the counter and dripping down the cupboards onto the floor. I'd forgotten to put the coffee pot under the spigot. What a mess!

My body is changing, and I do forget things. But sometimes forgetting is just due to lack of attention or too much multitasking, nothing more, and it doesn't dampen my enthusiasm about growing older. I felt excited about turning sixty and have felt excited ever since. I love this time of my life, spilled coffee and all. Besides, my forgetfulness makes my husband feel better now that he has company.

All in all I feel grateful. My eyes are more compromised than they once were, and I have more aches and pains than I'd like, but at the moment I'm not coping with other health or disability issues. I'm optimistic about the future and my ability to manage whatever comes my way. Apparently I'm in good company. My own research, like that of other senior authors, confirms that most people have a welcoming view of life after sixty.

The best is yet to come—I agree with other senior authors on that—though none of us ignores the real concerns of aging, including illness, pain, loss and grief. Our future depends on random events that we can't control, needless to say, but also on our perspective, which we can control. Our physical, emotional and spiritual well-being play a major role, of course, and they are a direct result of time we spend building our inner resources.

My long-time friend Trudy is just as excited about this time in her life despite her previous four years of serious health challenges. During those dark days, she talked about her problems and her pain, wept when she needed to, met each challenge head-on, dealt with it as best she could and carried on, some days bowed but definitely not broken. Her sunny disposition shone through all the pain, discomfort and discouragement, and she remained optimistic.

Her health issues sidelined her from work for almost a year, but she returned with a flourish—giving all to the work and people she loved. In 2009 her close friend and mentor died of cancer, and one year later so did her adopted son-in-law. During this time, Trudy reflected on what she would most regret not doing should her cancer return in the next few years. She realized that she wanted time. One priority was to spend time with her youngest grandchildren, who lived almost three thousand miles away. Another was to take time to be active and creative, have fun and do what she could to reclaim her good health. With mixed emotions, in September 2010, she chose to call it a day and took an indefinite sabbatical.

Recently she called me late one evening, too excited to sleep. Her six-month medical checkup was her best in four years. Trudy's doctor praised her approach to her illness, which had dramatically reduced the risk of her cancer returning. What did she do? In April 2011 she had moved across the country and began caring for her two young grandchildren, and began saying yes to things that were creative and fun.

Trudy's day begins at 5:30 a.m. when she gets up and goes off to a local gym for exercise and swimming. She then goes to her daughter and son-in-law's house to care for the children while Mum and Dad go out to work. She also prepares and shares the evening meal, which she manages to make fun. Crispy Wednesdays, when Trudy makes a fruit crisp for dessert, have become a tradition. In August 2011 she cycled the Cabot Trail with nine other people and their two guides. The high from that experience carried her for months, and she can't wait to have another adventure next year.

For her sixty-fifth birthday her family arranged a ride in a hot-air balloon. Her daughter, son and mother, Eileen, who was ninety-one, went up with her in her beautiful balloon. Trudy made a major course change and lives with gusto, fully engaged in her new life, getting younger by the day.

Cardiologist Mimi Guarneri, MD, told a story in her book *The Heart Speaks: A Cardiologist Reveals the Secret Language of Healing*. Paul, a middle-aged man with a wife and young child, had a heart attack due to three blocked arteries, which Dr. Guarneri opened during heart surgery. Having other risk factors for heart disease, he needed to change his diet, get more exercise and take a serious look at his stressful lifestyle or—the implication was clear—he might not live to see his child grow up. Dr. Guarneri told him, "You're on the tracks, and the train's coming. You can stand there or you can get off. It's your choice."

There is nothing like a stroke or heart attack to make us pay attention. As our arteries age, one in two of us will have hypertension by the age of sixty. Although this is a well-understood, measurable and treatable condition, many go on to have heart attacks, strokes or kidney failure.

Hypertension may be the Fagin of all silent thieves. Thankfully, the number of patients who suffer a stroke or heart attack is falling, largely as a consequence of better identification and treatment of hypertension.

Some stress is inevitable in a well-lived life. Each of us views stress differently and responds according to our age, maturity, emotional stability, physical activity, current health, sense of humour, past experience, family or other concerns, and basic personality. Calm people experience less stress than angry ones. Calm people don't get road rage. The older we get, the more calm we need in our lives. And sometimes we need to tack.

Tacking, to a sailor, means altering course; we're still heading in the same general direction but zigzagging toward it. When we tack, we pass through the eye of the wind, changing only our angle of approach. Sailing has taught me that the richest, quickest route to a distant shore is rarely a straight line. If we head too forcefully against a strong wind, we lose all forward momentum, get caught "in irons," standing stock still and making no headway. In order to reach any distant shore, however we define it, we need to know when to ease up and tack. Only then will we regain our perspective, pick up speed and sail triumphantly into a safe harbour.

In 1995 I started studying for my PhD in counselling psychology at the University of Victoria, a two-hour drive from my home. Twice a week I left about 6:30 a.m., drove to the university, attended meetings and lectures, used the library and typically turned for home twelve hours later. The trips both ways were in the dark, frequently in rain and occasionally in snow. Three and a half days a week I continued to see clients in my private practice. I studied during the other day and a half. Early on I developed dizzy spells and blurry vision, which I blithely ignored. Then I started getting headaches, stomach problems and frozen shoulder.

My doctor told me my symptoms were caused by stress, which I mightily resented at the time. I felt as though he was discounting my real physical ailments and telling me they were all in my head. In fact he was telling me that my body was protesting the amount of pressure I was subjecting it to, and that I'd best stop and pay attention. I wasn't yet ready to listen, since I was in denial. I was under considerable pressure to produce and perform, and I can't think of two more powerful stress-producing expectations.

Then one day I saw the train coming, to use Mimi Guarneri's analogy, and knew I had to get off the track. On my way to Victoria one morning after a snowfall, I hit an icy patch and turned a full circle on a four-lane highway, spinning across my two southbound lanes and the two northbound lanes, all fortunately empty of other cars. My car sailed off the highway to land safely upright in a ditch on a soft pillow of snow. I was unhurt, though no doubt in shock. I sat for quite a while expecting a passing motorist to stop, hoping to be rescued, but the top of my white car was invisible from up on the highway.

Eventually I stepped out of the car into knee-deep snow, climbed the embankment and walked to a farmhouse to call a towing company. The tow truck pulled my car, undented and unscratched, out of the ditch, and I carried on to my university lectures. Why on earth didn't I turn around and go home? At the time it never occurred to me. After dark that night I drove home, deep in thought, until with horror I saw my headlights dim and go out. Luckily I was close to our house. That day my guardian angels worked overtime.

Soon afterward Lou and I discussed my need to withdraw from my program. I told him, "If I were younger and single and lived in Victoria, perhaps I could do this."

Lou replied, "Well, we could arrange for you to be single, and then you could move to Victoria. But you can't be younger."

Some of us need to feel the rumble of the freight train before we see the light and get out of the way. I got off the track in February 1996, just ten months shy of my forty-ninth birthday—none too soon. The mere fact that I'm here to tell about it I consider to be a mini-miracle, and I'm grateful for it. I have no regrets.

Our circumstances and abilities change constantly as we grow and mature. If we want to remain fully in charge of our lives, we need regular review and redefinition of our priorities. This will pay rich dividends. It's always a delicate balancing act between blindly hanging on to a fading past and stepping purposefully forward to a bright future.

When I was nine, I received a small, forest-green autograph book. It had a thick quilted horizontal cover with creamy, smooth pages. I handed the book to various friends and family members, asking for their autograph. My Aunt Tee wrote, "Two men looked out of prison bars; one saw mud, the other stars. Motto: Always look on the bright side."

My eternal optimism may have sprung from this first seed. Now my life philosophy helps me read the wind and know when to make a course change.

12

Silent thieves

One October weekend a few years ago my brother, Ferg, his wife, Joy, our son Marty and daughter-in-law Kathy visited for Thanksgiving.

Marty and Kathy had noticed a whine in the overhead rack of their new car at highway speeds. Lou has always prided himself on his uncanny ability to diagnose mechanical problems by listening to machinery in operation. Kathy, Ferg and Lou went for a drive, and when they reached highway speeds, both Ferg and Kathy could hear the whine. Lou couldn't. Fortunately their clear description let him figure out and repair the problem, but there was no more denying that Lou couldn't hear as well as he used to.

Ironically I got an inkling the same weekend of how things are for people who have difficulty hearing or making themselves understood. Coming down with a cold, I felt as though my head was stuffed with cotton hay and rags.

Lou is a gourmet cook, and I was helping him prepare Coquilles St. Jacques for our Thanksgiving dinner. He'd filled a small pastry bag with hot mashed potatoes and was delicately piping potatoes around the edges of the scallop shells when the bag burst. Hot mashed potatoes spewed everywhere. It was one of those moments when you either laugh or cry. Lou and I laughed.

Soon I began to cough, and by the time I was finished, my throat was raw and sore and my voice was no more. For the next few days I couldn't talk and could barely hear. How frustrating for me and others! I wrote notes, many of which began with the plea, "Please look at me when talking and speak up."

In the winter of 2009, I discussed denial as it applies to hearing loss with Jon Cockcroft, a knowledgeable and compassionate hearing specialist in Parksville, British Columbia. Jon told me that his clinic patients regularly say, "My hearing is just fine. Everyone else, my wife included, mumbles." Jon added that it takes about seven years from the time a person notices something wrong with their hearing to the point where they're willing to do anything about it. Meanwhile, their hearing continues to deteriorate. Thanks to Jon's expertise, encouragement and ongoing support, Lou now wears hearing aids, and his life is infinitely richer.

For at least seven years I noticed that Lou couldn't hear as well as in the past, but all my comments literally fell on deaf ears. I know from talking with others, particularly women, that this is more the norm than the exception. All that changed in the fall of

2007, not because of anything I said, but because of Lou's own disconcerting experience in trying to diagnose that car problem. Our own experience is the ultimate teacher.

Hearing loss may be even more frustrating for those of us living with people who are hard of hearing when they refuse to get their hearing tested, deny that they don't hear properly, or after being tested and diagnosed, still refuse to wear their hearing aids. I personally know of at least five people, four elderly men and one woman, who each invested thousands of dollars in hearing aids only to regularly leave them out. It's challenging and awkward to carry on any meaningful conversation with them; they can't hear well, and without their aids, lip reading goes only so far. They smile and nod as if in agreement, but frequently they're not sure exactly what has been said and soon feel disconnected. Tragically, they withdraw into themselves, and their worlds shrink prematurely. Others, not knowing how to effectively communicate, withdraw from them.

Social situations involving more than two people seem to be the most challenging. I have observed insensitivity to people who are hard of hearing and believe it's inadvertent rather than intentional. In the rapid give-and-take of conversation we may often only half listen. If people are courageous enough to say they're hard of hearing, it doesn't register; if it does register, we may speak up for a minute or two and then quickly forget, defaulting to our usual way of speaking. We may not mumble, but we may also not articulate clearly enough or pay sufficient attention to our listeners to ensure they've heard what we said. The more people talking, the more difficult it is to separate specific sounds from the background noise.

Probably the world's most famous blind person, Helen Keller, wrote in a letter to Dr. James Kerr Love in 1910, "I am just as deaf as I am blind. The problems of deafness are deeper and more complex, if not more important, than those of blindness. Deafness is a much worse misfortune. For it means the loss of the most vital stimulus—the sound of the voice that brings language, sets thought astir, and keeps us in the intellectual company of [people]." Sound also makes possible the joy of listening to music, birdsong, rain on the roof, a crackling fire or the laughter of children.

Adjusting to hearing aids is far more difficult than adjusting to continuous bifocals, in my observation. Yet I never have been able to adjust to continuous bifocals—they make me dizzy—so I continue to put my reading glasses on and off throughout the day. This wouldn't work well for hearing aids. In the beginning they also can make users dizzy and disoriented as their brains and ears learn to process sounds differently. Jon Cockcroft told me this can take at least two to three months.

I admire Lou's determination and tenacity and am infinitely grateful for Jon's follow-up and patience. In the beginning Lou went to Jon's office once a week, then monthly, for a long time. Three years later Lou switched to more sophisticated digital hearing aids, which also require regular cleaning and adjustment to either the hearing aid itself or the little tubes that run into his ears. The initial cost of the hearing aids covers all this.

It's essential, when we take that first tentative step to find a hearing specialist, to ask if the cost of the hearing aid covers ongoing service. If we feel we're a burden or are being two-bitted to death every time a hearing aid needs adjustment, which may be frequently as we grow and change, we're unlikely to return. Many seniors are concerned about asking for extra service and simply don't; expensive hearing aids end up in dresser drawers while the owners withdraw more and more to a world without sound. Our horizons can easily and unexpectedly shrink.

When I had cataract surgery (see Chapter 2: Aloneness), I felt lucky and relieved to be called in after a last-minute cancellation. My surgeon successfully extracted my cataract and implanted a new lens. Adjusting to the new lens for the first few days reminded me of my experience with continuous bifocals. I coped with a side-to-side flutter, rather than an up-and-down one, but this quickly passed, and all is now well.

Coincidentally my dear eighty-nine-year-old Aunt Edna had cataract surgery the same day as I did. When I spoke with her on the phone, she was delighted that she could now sit three feet from her computer and read it clearly—without glasses.

Cataracts, glaucoma and age-related macular degeneration are all silent thieves. They creep up ever so slowly, and left unchecked, they do irreversible damage to the eyes. Hearing aids provide assistance, but they don't reverse hearing loss. And certain hearing-loss conditions, I understand, don't improve with hearing aids.

Let's not take the gift of sight and hearing for granted! What we take for granted, sadly, we ignore. Any substantial reduction in sight, hearing or any of our senses will severely limit our ability to energetically explore our world and fully engage in our lives.

Touch enabled Helen Keller's teacher, Anne Sullivan, to begin communicating with her. It's fascinating to watch films showing their one-handed, fingers-flying conversation. Helen learned to speak by holding her hand on Anne's face—she could pick up different vibrations transmitted by Anne's throat, lips and facial bones—and eventually learned her first letters and sounds. Her particularly poignant example reminds us of how her world opened up through her fingertips.

Today I am housebound, since winter snowstorms turned to driving rain and freezing ice that made walking treacherous. The snow and ice are melting quickly, but it's only a few days since my cataract surgery, and the wind is too cold to brave. So I stand in my backyard and view my surroundings, near and far, through a new lens.

Details and definition, edges and outlines, fascinate me. Pockets of grainy white snow rest between brilliant-green moss-covered rocks. I catch a flash of iridescent green as a rufous hummingbird whizzes between one branch and another bereft of any sweet-smelling flower. For a brief moment it alights on the peach-red leaves of a nandina bush and just as quickly flies off to find more succulent nectar. I hear the hollow, cupped call of a raven perched high in a nearby arbutus tree and see a hint of black as he disappears into the woods.

Tall fir trees stand in bold outline before puffy clouds. The distant hills look far more crisp than they did a week ago. I appreciate the overcast, which lets me gaze at the clouds without sunglasses. Do you remember lying on your back in a field as a child, looking up and seeing pictures in the clouds? Do you remember picking out faces and animals and watching horses gallop across the cloudy skies? I do. Today, as I study the clouds, a tableau unfolds before my eyes: the suggestion of a grey-and-white Chinese brush painting of a person with two little dogs standing on a beach and looking off to the distant horizon of trees and mountains. A clear path of ever-changing shapes appears as the clouds drift across the sky, and it opens up with patches of blue and slivers of sunlight. The sky is full of possibility and promise, and my world is once again settled and clear.

We experience our world through our senses. Sight, sound, smell, touch and taste give our lives texture, delight and adventure. Some deterioration of our senses is inevitable as we age, but let's not allow any sense to slip away for lack of attention. I'm all for stemming the tide as long as we can, grieving as we need to, celebrating our amazing ability to adapt and moving on.

13

CREATIVE VOICE

HISTORY AND HOPE HANG ON my family room wall. When I gaze at the still life painting that Lou and I bought for twenty-five dollars more than forty years ago, that's what I see. We've hung this original oil painting proudly in every home since, and after a move or renovation I never feel quite settled until this painting is up. The history embodies part of our early life together; the hope reflects the artist who painted it. I can never consider the painting without remembering the painter, and when I touch it, I feel as though I'm gently touching the painter's hands or eyes and expressing my years of ongoing gratitude.

Picture an old Chianti bottle topped with a small, well-used cork; someone obviously recorked this bottle a few times before the artist captured it in this painting. The pale-green bottle rests solidly in its blond straw basket. Just left and forward sits an oval royal-blue bowl beside a rust-coloured candlestick about three-quarters the height of the bottle. A brilliant red apple, looking good enough to eat, anchors the bottom left corner of the painting. Just right and forward of the basket is a scalloped, burgundy-coloured vase and in front of that a bright yellow lemon. An onion in its skin, with its long, curved green top still attached, snuggles into a corner of the earthen-coloured blanket that provides a backdrop for this artwork.

The entire picture is embraced by a thick, concave, grey-and-white frame with gold trim. Friends regularly remark on the beauty of the painting; it is eye-catching. The artist clearly had command of his subject. His use of light gives the entire scene depth and character.

But who was the artist? The painting is unsigned, and we never met the painter. At the time I was working as a volunteer with developmentally challenged and physically disabled adults under the auspices of Arbutus Crafts in Victoria. Physically handicapped youths and adults were more invisible and mar-ginalized forty years ago than they are today. They lived in the shadows.

Every spring Arbutus Crafts brought together the arts and crafts produced throughout the year for an annual show. The sixteen-by-twenty-inch painting caught our eye soon after we walked into the room. It was masterfully displayed, all by itself, on a large easel that stood in front and to the right of the stage. I can still feel the excitement and enthusiasm of the artist's friends as they protectively mingled around his creation. He wasn't there that evening; he was too severely disabled even to attend the art classes at the centre. Physically disabled he may have been, but artistically he was more than able. I can imagine that more than anything he wanted to be recognized not for his disability but for his real talent and skills.

When Lou and I purchased his painting, the volunteers and other students treated us like royalty. This had to be a big event for any artist—the sale of his first painting—and his friends made a point of letting us know just how much it would mean to this artist. I was thrilled that our genuine enjoyment of his painting would help this courageous young man. Creating anything of lasting beauty requires discipline and devotion to one's art, and he was obviously off to a good start.

This artist's story inspires me. When I hear clients or friends with good eyesight and strong hands disparage their own attempts to create art, I think of this young man and his endless hours of struggle. I want to tell them, find your own means of expression, devote the necessary time, stick with it, hone your skills and follow your heart. Treasure, respect and share your gift. The world needs it. Ignore destructive criticism. So much talent is stifled, and so many voices are stilled, by cruel criticism from others who lack reverence for the creative and original. Creativity is inclusive; it's open to us all.

Perhaps as a child you dreamed of becoming an artist—a painter, weaver, musician, writer, cartoonist or maker of fine furniture—but life intervened, and consciously or unaware you consigned your dream to the background of your life. Now is the time to bring it forward and unearth forgotten hopes and talents.

Some fortunate few discover their particular passion early in life and have the good sense to keep it front and centre. My friend Page Ough would argue that she had no choice; her painting talent has held her enthralled for more than fifty years. It's been my privilege to watch Page paint and hear at first hand her reverence and gratitude for her gift. She approaches each new painting as an adventure. We share an affinity for long periods of solitude and silence: she with her acrylics and canvas, birds and bears, me with my pen and paper or flying fingers on the computer keyboard, weaving words into stories.

Page is as comfortable in the woods, by the sea or in the mountains as most of us are in the safety of our houses. The seasons inspire her daily, each with its own jewels that she brings alive on canvas. Page particularly loves all the wild animals of the Rocky Mountains and captures their magnificent vitality with her brush.

She goes where she can see the bears in their natural habitat in the Bugaboo region, high up in the Purcell Mountains in the British Columbia Interior, accessible only by helicopter. On one trip the pilot dropped her and her husband, Michael, in a mountain meadow after telling them, "This is where the bears come to eat the wildflowers." Now she paints all her bears with flowers in their mouths.

As she paints, Page listens to CDs of inspiring speakers. She lent me a few for my 2010 drive to Los Gatos, and I was fortunate to pick them up just before she shipped her latest creations off to the gallery in Banff, Alberta. The large black eyes of her life-sized bears gazed at me from the canvas, their mouths full of flowers. I was mesmerized, and tears came to my eyes; the bears looked so alive that I wanted to reach out and touch them.

Expressing her quirky sense of humour, Page usually paints her flowers with a land snail, ladybug or butterfly cheekily perched on leaf or petal. Her colourful parrot tulips fairly dance on the canvas, inviting us to pick them and put them in a crystal vase in the sunshine. Her paintings tantalize the senses, and they enshrine her unending love affair with nature, all the birds of the air and the creatures of land and sea.

Over the years I've tried my hand at sketching, woodcarving, Chinese calligraphy and brush painting, and more recently, thanks to Page's patient teaching, painting with acrylics. I most enjoy sketching; I love the smell of pencil crayons, their soft, muted colours and the smooth feel of pencil sliding on paper. No amount of practice or dedication will ever produce anything more than the hours of enjoyment I get from the process. It is a relaxing and worthwhile hobby, and that is enough.

One artistic form that I recently discovered, however, results in creations beautiful enough to share. It's also enlightening and great fun.

My friend Barbara is an adventurer who sometimes entices me to share her journeys into the unknown. In the fall of 2008 she introduced me to SoulCollage, which combines art, self-discovery and community building. After her brief introduction I purchased *SoulCollage: An Intuitive Collage Process for Individuals and Groups* by Seena B. Frost and went wild. Within a few short months I'd made sixty vivid and imaginative—to my eye—works of art. I was hooked. In the spring of 2009 Barbara and I travelled to Seattle to train as SoulCollage facilitators and both returned eager to share with others our new-found sense of wonder.

SoulCollage is an inspired and generous gift to the world by Seena B. Frost, a petite, white-haired sage who holds master's degrees in psychology and divinity. Seena turned eighty in 2012 and continues to write and teach. She extols and epitomizes the rich treasures we can uncover through honouring our creative voice. The more we create and expand ourselves, the more we'll have to share with the world. I met her in 2009 at a SoulCollage conference in Tubac, Arizona, and was fortunate to share and discuss many of my cards with her during the Three Faces of Silence retreat in Los Gatos (see Chapter 3: Silence invites reflection). Like Seena, I gain a great deal of personal satisfaction from introducing others to this remarkable process.

In SoulCollage we arrange, then glue down, images gathered from old photos, books, magazines and calendars onto five-by-eight-inch mat board cards. While making these one-of-a-kind cards, we soon learn that every one of us is an artist and each card is a personal, enduring work of art that's not for sale, barter or trade.

It is easy to underestimate the complexity and power of SoulCollage. Pick out any image from any magazine, calendar or photograph. Let your imagination trip freely through the images—animal, bird, bug, flower, friend or inspirational figure—to which you are drawn. And then, with childlike courage and curiosity, step into and speak from the image. Let go of any adult constraints. Listen to what you say. Write it down. The discoveries are fascinating.

Imagine how inspiring it can be to choose an image of a relative or friend whom we particularly admire. Then for a moment we take on the characteristics of our chosen teacher and raise her voice in our own words. Seena suggests we begin all such statements first with "I am the one who—" We may say, "I am the one who laughs at the irony in life; I am the one who does not take myself too seriously; I am the one who reaches out to others . . ." If we periodically pull this card and set it up on a shelf, its image may remind us to be lighthearted and considerate of others. In this way we can make no end of heartwarming connections with ourselves, friends, relatives, colleagues and neighbours.

The more images we work with, the more personal cards we create, the more we learn about ourselves. We learn not only how we view the world but also the place we've carved for ourselves in our world. Every card tells a part of our own story. I now have over a hundred cards and regularly draw on them for inspiration and guidance grounded in people who have positively influenced my life, coupled with my own experience and intuition. They are a joy to use and behold, and I love passing on the process to kindred spirits.

Writing is my daily passionate outlet, of course, and I have struggled long and hard to hone my craft. Doubt accompanies every chapter, and I wonder always if the words and stories and metaphors will come. Over the years I've abandoned this love and found my life sorely lacking. In the process I've discovered that I can't not write. That, I believe, is the key. What we need to do is what we can't not do. When we cut ourselves off from our creative voice, we cut ourselves off from our own source, and our life pales.

We all need to rediscover reverence and wonder through a creative outlet—baking or gardening, painting or writing, singing or dancing—whatever brings sparkle into your life. Each of us has a creative voice that we need to raise. We are all artists at heart!

Part IV

Anchors in the Wind

14

ONE MAGICAL EVENING

KINDNESS CREATES MAGIC, WHICH CASTS a long-lasting glow.

Life at our house could be unpredictable. On the morning of the church Christmas bazaar and turkey dinner, before Mum and Dad left for work, the plan was for my brother, Fergus, and I to attend that evening. All day I kept hoping we could go, but not too much, just in case it didn't work out. Mum and Dad might be too tired, or a blizzard might strike windy, snowy Calgary in the dark days of winter.

Our Lady of Perpetual Help's church hall stood at the bottom of a long, twisty road in Northeast Calgary. We lived on a hill a few miles away, so either Mum or Dad would have to drive us. They both came home in a good mood! And Dad offered to drive us to the bazaar.

The hall perched right on the sidewalk, and a lone bulb over the door cast a wide, yellow glow out into the street, just like the street lamp in one of my favourite stories, *The Little Match*

Girl. The night was windy, dark and bitterly cold. Great white puffs of exhaust rose in clouds behind all the cars. Dad was able to pull up right in front and let us off, so Ferg and I hopped out of the car, skipped across the sidewalk and ran up the few steps to the door.

We stepped into another world full of warm, happy people. The air crackled with excitement, and everybody seemed to be talking at once and hugging each other. Those who'd walked some distance were stamping their feet to knock the snow off their boots, leaving big muddy puddles on the floor. Bodies pressed together, jostling one another, as adults and kids wiggled out of layers of clothes. The air was steamy with the smell of wet wool.

My brother, older than me by three and a half years, had instructions to take care of me, and of course he didn't. This was perfectly okay with me. I'd just turned eight and could take care of myself. But the entranceway was crowded, and I couldn't undo the big buttons or the belt on my hand-me-down, too-long blue overcoat. The belt never stayed tied when I wanted it to, but Mum had pulled it tight as I headed out the door, and now there was no getting it undone. I couldn't budge it, try as I might, and Ferg had long since disappeared into the crowd.

I must have looked a tad forlorn as I squeezed my way out of the cloakroom, glancing around for a familiar face. I stood right beside a big table that overflowed with coats, hats, mitts and scarves, but nobody seemed to notice that I still wore my coat.

Maybe they thought I was cold. Maybe they didn't even see me. I wasn't about to ask a stranger for help, so I just kept fiddling with my belt.

And then, over the din of voices, I heard my name and looked up into the dancing, dark eyes of Mrs. Dandurand. She was wearing a red-and-white Santa hat over her soft, brown hair, and the white pompom bounced beside her tiny face. Her olive skin felt smooth against my cold cheek as she knelt in front of me and gave me a big hug. It felt good, though we didn't hug much in our family, and I was glad to see her. Until this evening I'd only met Mrs. Dandurand at church on Sunday mornings and once last summer at our house. She'd brought over her daughter Toni's old bicycle for me to ride.

Mrs. Dandurand had seen Fergus but not Mum and Dad, and seemed surprised when I told her Mum was home with my little sister, Liz, and Dad had dropped us off. But she just set about untying my knotted belt and helped me off with my coat. She made sure my mitts and hat were securely stuck in the pocket and added my coat to the pile on the table.

Santa's helper, my rescuer, tried to tidy my thick, unruly blonde hair. Most of it was drawn back into a long braid, and there really wasn't much to be done about all the flyaway, sticky-out bits that surrounded my freckled face. After a pat and a tuck, she just chuckled and smiled and said it looked fine.

Everyone had to pass through the main hallway where we stood between the kitchen on our left, the cloakroom on our right and the bazaar straight ahead. Mrs. Dandurand was a one-woman welcoming committee, the quintessential warm-hearted Italian mother. I happily basked in her kindness.

Collaring my brother as he ran by, she led us both toward the kitchen. It was the Christmas bazaar and turkey dinner, after all; both parts were equally important. Mrs. Dandurand was chief cook and organizer of the dinner, which cost a dollar. It never occurred to her that we weren't having her turkey dinner. Everyone had the dinner! I swear I saw her dark amber eyes flash and a cloud pass across her sweet face when Ferg told her we each had twenty-five cents for the bazaar but no dinner tickets. She lost some of her forward momentum, but not much and not for long. She simply took my hand, kept her other one on my brother's shoulder and continued to guide us into the kitchen. When Ferg hesitated, she said not to worry, she would talk with Mum later. It was clear she intended to feed us, ticket or no.

She made a place for us at one end of a long table. Lots of other kids and adults were sitting there, and most of them knew my brother. He played hockey and served Mass as an altar boy every Sunday, and some of the kids were in his class. I didn't see anyone from my class, but then I was only in grade two in a new school, and unlike my popular brother, I preferred the sidelines. I was content just to watch, listen—and smell.

The aroma was glorious, particularly the aroma of roasting turkey. Turkey—unlike roast beef with its heavy, meaty aroma—smells light, fresh and utterly delectable. We didn't wait long before Mrs. Dandurand brought our turkey dinner. And what a dinner it was! Each of us had a small piece of dark meat, a large slice of white meat, an ice-cream-scoop mound of stuffing and another of mashed potatoes, plus a large spoonful of peas and carrots. A wide river of taffy-coloured, smooth, silky gravy wound over it all.

Never before had I seen such a feast. Not only did it look inviting, it smelled divine and tingled every taste bud on my tongue. There wasn't a lump in the mashed potatoes, and the white meat was moist instead of shoe-leather dry. Even the peas and carrots tasted sweet. It was truly mouth-watering. I took my time, even dawdled. It wasn't that I didn't want to eat. I just wanted to drag out the moment and savour every delicious, tasty morsel.

Ferg finished long before me and joined the other kids lining up to get their little dessert bags from Santa. When he talked with Santa, he pointed at me. I don't know what he said, but I imagine that he told Santa I was too shy to come up and get my own bag and asked for one for me. Maybe this was his way of taking care of me. He dropped my bag on the table and took off again with his friends. He was an okay big brother, as brothers go.

Dessert was in a red drawstring bag shaped like a small stocking with a candy cane sticking out of the top. It was filled with goodies such as chocolate bells, each wrapped in shiny red or green or gold paper, cookies wrapped in wax paper, hard Christmas candy—including my favourite ribbon twists—and a mandarin orange stuffed in the toe. Treasure!

I was wide-eyed with wonder as I looked around and breathed in all the good feelings floating by on the air. It was like a big, noisy dream. Talk and laughter mingled with the sound of chairs scraping across the floor and the clatter of dishes as people moved around getting their dinner or coffee.

Soon Mrs. Dandurand, my guardian angel, came by with her own coffee and a plate of Christmas cookies. She'd seen that Ferg wasn't going to spend much time with his little sister; perhaps she'd also noticed that I didn't know anyone and was a bit shy, or perhaps she just liked me. When she came by to see how I was doing, she'd pat my hair or brush my cheek, always giving me a big smile. Whatever the reason, it warmed me right down to my toes. Among all these strangers, I felt safe.

After I helped her clear off some of the dishes, holding tight to my treasure bag, we made our way to the bazaar. A few tables along the wall had items for sale such as pies and cookies, cakes and breads, jams, jellies and jars of fruit and vegetables. Other tables held knitted sweaters, hats, mitts, socks and scarves or were stacked with aprons, tablecloths and fancy knitted dolls. Mrs. Dandurand stopped and talked to most of the people at the tables as we went by.

I couldn't wait to get to the fish pond, which was easy to spot because it had the longest lineup of kids. Big pieces of cardboard jutted out from a wall, decorated with drawings of funny-looking fish and a big number 5 followed by a little C with a slash through it. A try at the fish pond cost five cents. On the table in front lay two or three bendy bamboo poles with string tied to the end and a large safety pin knotted on the end of the string. When it was my turn, I held onto the end of the pole, and one of Santa's helpers put the string over the top of the cardboard. The bamboo pole wiggled and jerked—just like I imagined it would with a real fish—and when I gave it a tug, out it popped with a brown bag pinned to the end. Every bag contained a surprise. I loved the fish pond.

The first time I fished, I hooked a brown bag containing an O'Henry chocolate bar, but I was far too stuffed to eat it and just put it into my dessert bag for later. Then I had to wait while the other kids fished. Mrs. Dandurand went into the fish pond to help out, and the next time I fished, the brown bag contained a tiny package with ten jacks and a small red rubber ball. My third and final time was the absolute best. I couldn't believe my eyes when I opened the brown bag and pulled out a tiny, soft, knitted doll, almost small enough to fit in my pocket. It was pale blue with a tiny white face, black stitching for the eyes and upturned mouth, and a wee button nose. Framing its face were bangs of yellow wool, and it had a short yellow braid tied with a red ribbon.

I didn't play much with dolls, but this wasn't a playing-with kind of doll, and it wouldn't last long if my little sister got her sticky hands on it. It was soft and precious, and I would give it a place of honour on top of my dresser, right at the back below the window. Mrs. Dandurand seemed just as thrilled as I was about the little doll, and we both continued to admire it as we wandered away from the fish pond.

I'd looked forward to this bazaar all day without any idea of what to expect, and now it was drawing to a close. I don't know what I would have done without Mrs. Dandurand. She'd taken me under her wing for the whole evening, shared my delight in my new doll, and when Dad came to pick us up, helped me on with my coat and made sure I was all bundled up against the cold night. Then she hugged me close and said goodbye.

Kindness is a gift. We can't buy it or earn it. It comes unbidden and catches us by surprise, leaving a warm glow. How do we thank someone for the lifelong gift of a lifetime? If you asked me to colour her gift of kindness, I would paint a double rainbow reaching from one horizon to the other, with generous splashes of turquoise, magenta, rosy pink, flaming orange and purple, gently fading to the softest lavender mauve. And in the middle would be a banner reading, Thank You, Mrs. Dandurand.

15

A WELCOME TOUCH

W ELCOME," SAID ELEANOR—TALL, SILVER-HAIRED AND elegant—as she reached out a graceful hand to touch me on the knee.

A hundred of us sat crammed into a church hall to listen to a speaker sponsored by the business and professional club to which Eleanor and my husband, Lou, belong. As Lou's guest that day, I knew only a few people. Eleanor's gesture warmed my heart, and I relaxed. Did she realize that something that came so naturally to her meant a lot to me? It reminded me of a similar gesture I'd made months earlier to make someone else feel welcome.

Lou sings in a local men's chorus, and I occasionally find myself sitting in slowly filling churches or theatres, waiting for the performance to begin. I always bring a book and immerse myself in my own little world, head down and oblivious to what goes on around me. In a crowd it doesn't come naturally to me to approach other people.

One evening in the winter of 2010 I sat in St. Andrew's Church in downtown Nanaimo, British Columbia. This 115-year-old church has particularly grand acoustics and is a favourite venue for choral performances. The wooden pews are equally old and as uncomfortable as you'd expect. They were filling quickly, and as I squirmed and shifted around to get comfortable, I noticed an elderly woman walking up the aisle. She looked a bit lost despite her smart blue-grey jacket and slacks and close-cropped brown hair, so I asked her if she was looking for someone. She was looking for a good seat, she said, and I motioned to the one beside me, moving my books so she could sit.

Soon the performance began. Toward the end of the first half, the conductor asked the audience to join in the singing, and a beautiful, resonant voice emanated from my seating companion. I sat entranced. What a gift to hear her sing! During the intermission we discussed singing. New to the mid-Island area, she hoped to join a choir, so—to her excitement—I told her the Island Soul Choir welcomed all comers. At the end of the performance we thanked each other for gifts given and received.

Every time I take a chance and step out of my comfort zone, I've noticed, I'm blessed with these unexpected gifts. The rewards far outweigh the risks.

It's not easy to be a shy senior. In fact it's not easy for anyone to be reserved and awkward in groups of people, familiar or not. Mingling in social situations and engaging in chit-chat can be painful and difficult for shy people. As we age, it's all too easy to make less and less effort, which will inevitably lead to more social isolation. We feel as though safety lies in solitude, not in numbers. Men and women who reach out and offer a welcome, as Eleanor did, pave the way for shy people to actively participate.

The underlying issue for the shy and reserved, I believe, is fear of standing out in any way that draws unwelcome attention. We either talk too much and say the wrong thing, then blush like the devil, or we get tongue-tied. I sometimes wish that I got tongue-tied more often. Childhood experiences of humiliation may linger just below the surface of our consciousness. While they may prick us every now and then, they remain largely discounted and ignored as contributing factors to our reluctance to reach out.

I can still feel the face-burning shame of being strapped for talking in line when I was in grade one. And I well remember being absolutely mortified during a university debating competition before a large University of Waterloo audience when my smart-mouthed remark about a fellow debater backfired and left me looking foolish.

They weren't even my words; someone else had added them to my speech, and I'd assumed they knew best what would enhance my debating position. What a mistake! What I said was, "Ye gods, I think I have just been hit by the jawbone of an ass." The experienced and erudite debater from Royal Military College, Kingston—a handsome, dark-haired, young man—simply said, "And you look like it too!"

I will never forget either of those experiences, though I no longer attach any emotion to them, and neither one holds me back today. They did teach me useful lessons. My strapping certainly gave me a deep distrust of authority and an intense need to explain myself and be understood. My debating blooper now makes me laugh, but it also taught me that I'm not good at quick repartee, a lesson reinforced over the years. From that moment on I've written all my own material and had it well edited. Good editors can protect writers from heart-stopping blunders.

Many of us had similar experiences in our youth or young adult years. If they still cause anxiety and tears, we resist reaching out to others and engaging in a full social life. We need to take them out of our backpack, expose them to the light of today, absorb their valuable gifts and let go of the angst. It can be a freeing, uplifting experience, well worth a try.

Fortunately, with the wisdom of our senior years, we tend to worry less about what others think of us and therefore are less likely to feel embarrassed. This is one of my true joys in moving through my sixties. We can also hope to be stronger, wiser and perhaps more resilient as a result of our experiences. It is a truism that some of our best lessons come from our most painful moments. We don't forget them, but if we're lucky, they leave us with funny or poignant stories to relate. Our senior years help us more easily forget ourselves. We can take a chance and shift our focus from our own fear of embarrassment to wondering what we can do to bring a smile to someone else's face. When we step out of the shadow of shyness, we step into a lighter, more socially engaged future that helps us grow. It's also a lot more fun.

There are many ways to reach out and touch someone; even complete strangers do it. After I fell on the beach—bruising my tailbone, giving myself a headache and badly straining my wrist (see Chapter 10: My body, my friend)—I stopped at our local grocery store to pick up two litres of milk, a couple of newspapers, green beans, bananas and a few tins of Belgian hazelnut instant coffee.

I picked up a red plastic basket and foolishly hung the two black handles over my right wrist. By the time I got to the checkout line, my wrist was aching and I wanted to quickly unload my groceries. But someone had left the handles up on the top basket in the stack, so I couldn't put down my basket. With my heavy purse slipping off my left shoulder and my frustration growing, I precariously perched the basket on the end of the counter and yanked out each item, half dropping them on the now moving conveyor belt. Then I was able to bang open the handles on the offending basket and none too quietly drop my basket into it, finally relieving the strain on my sore wrist.

A tall, cherubic stranger in a wrinkled, blue duffle coat and a sailor's cap stood ahead of me in line, grinning. "You're feeling cranky."

"I am not," I shot back. Then I took a good look at the twinkle in his eyes, poked him in the arm, smiled and said, "Well, maybe a little. What made you think so?"

With a wide grin he said, "Because of how you unloaded your groceries."

By then we were both laughing. He paid his bill, we wished each other a good day and he was off.

How many grinning strangers have you encountered who would reach out and touch someone in a similar manner? He took a risk, and I was able to respond to his teasing voice and smiling face. I've never seen him before or since, but this delightful human connection continues to make me smile.

Nanoose Bay is a special Island community. People reach out and take care of each other, including the warm-hearted staff of our local post office. They are unfailingly courteous and helpful, doing their best to ensure our mail is sent the most economical and efficient way possible. And where else would you find a constantly full dish of jelly beans or jujubes for those of us with a sweet tooth to nibble on while waiting to pick up or send mail? I love it.

One day as I approached the counter, a frail, elderly man shuffled slowly in the door to stand awkwardly bent in front of the post office boxes. He fumbled for his key. Maggie came out from behind the counter, walked over to greet him by name and touched him gently on the shoulder. Inclining her head to the side to study his face, she asked in a soft voice how he was doing. He shook his bowed head as a small tear slid down his lined cheek. "Not so well," he said. "Mary is in hospital again, and I am worried."

Maggie opened her arms and gathered him into a hug. Then she gently took his key, checked his box and gave him his mail. He took a deep breath, thanked her, gathered himself together—head now up—and walked out of the post office, buoyed by human kindness. She acknowledged his presence, saw his distress and conveyed compassion with a touch. Maggie gave him dignity.

16

GENEROSITY

OUR WORLD NEEDS MORE ECCENTRICS like my grand-uncle Pete. He harvested his resources and contributed greatly in his own way. He is my unsung hero, and telling you about him is my way of thanking him posthumously. If his generous act plants a seed for any of us to consider as we harvest our own resources, that would be a bonus.

Pete was a hermit, so I can claim that my love of solitude runs in the family, but I thank him for much more than that. He was the brother of my disagreeable grandfather, my father's father. I'm not surprised they grew apart. Pete didn't have much contact with his niece or two other nephews, just my father. Dad and Pete had a relationship based on good conversation and an occasional game of chess. Pete had eight grandnieces and four grandnephews, and as far as I know, I'm the only one of the twelve who met Pete.

One day when I was no more than thirteen, my father and I drove north from Calgary for about two and a half hours to

Ponoka to visit Pete. His home was a small cabin; that would be a generous word for the rough shack that stood on the side of a hill. Pete, a weather-wizened farmer, wore a wrinkled, grease-stained, cream shirt and baggy trousers held up by suspenders. His whiskery stubble sparkled in the sunlight, and he probably still had a full head of hair; that runs in the family too. I remember my grand-uncle warmly. Pete smelled, but his eyes smiled. He proudly showed us his large garden, fenced in chicken wire, and the small chicken coop at the back. My father said Pete prided himself on his self-sufficiency.

Pete lived alone and avoided people. When he died, my Dad cleared out his cabin. He found uncashed pension cheques, dividend cheques, Canada Savings Bonds and cash stuffed in cupboards, behind cracked picture frames, in broken teapots and under the mattress. If anyone had asked Pete his financial worth, I doubt he could have answered accurately. But he'd obviously given much thought to his legacy.

Pete left money to each of his grandnieces and grandnephews. Each of us received a small monthly cheque for twenty years from our twenty-first birthday until we turned forty-one. He would never know—or perhaps he does—the silent thank-yous directed heavenward month after month, year after year, by a handful of starving students, more than one single mother and other young parents like Lou and me on a shoestring budget. When the last nephew turned forty-one, the balance of the estate reverted to the University of Alberta to fund research into heart disease. I'd like to think that research assured a positive outcome for both Lou and Ferg, who each had a heart attack only a year apart; both are thriving five and six years later.

Pete inspires me. He was one of the quiet, unassuming people in our midst who give generously without thought of thanks or even acknowledgement. Thoughtful gifts have a ripple effect. They make a difference.

Contributing gives lifelong meaning and purpose to our lives. This only intensifies in our senior years, I believe, because we're hard-wired to contribute. We need to be needed; we need to be valued just as we are. Sometimes we forget that or mistakenly think we have nothing left to give, and then life loses its luster. But now that we've lived more than half a century, we have more skills, talents, abilities and experience to draw on than ever before in our lives. There are uncounted worthwhile ways—large and small, tangible and intangible—to contribute.

Our friend Bent is in his mid-sixties, so we weren't surprised when he retired for medical reasons. Then we saw him again, in the spring of 2011, getting set to work on an engine at a local marina.

As usual Bent was happy to lay down his tools and chat. He'd abandoned his retirement and returned to work in his cluttered workshop. Once again the large, big-hearted Dane is a familiar figure on the docks of local marinas. A master mechanic, he holds strong opinions about life in general and in particular anything relating to marine diesel engines. Generous with his extensive knowledge, he works at his own pace, and woe betide pushy customers. You wouldn't want to get Bent's dander up if he has your engine in pieces on his workbench. Lou gets along well with Bent, fortunately, because in recent years Bent has overhauled one marine diesel engine for us and installed two on our sailboat. One installation was in the middle of the summer, traditionally the busiest time of the year, but thanks to Bent, we didn't lose an entire cruising season.

In retirement he'd soon become bored and decided he was too young to retire. No doubt Bent truly missed the challenge of solving mechanical problems as well as his stimulating and often controversial conversations with his customers. He has much yet to contribute.

Lou was also weary when he retired from his company at sixty-nine, but now he consults part-time and thoroughly enjoys it. Like him and Bent, I'm grateful to continue with work that I find challenging and engaging. When I closed my counselling, consulting and psychotherapy practice at the end of 2006, I had lost my spark. I was tired, but I never considered that I was permanently retiring. I needed time to rest, reflect and shift perspectives from one way of working and contributing to another. And now I'm back at it: writing, coaching and facilitating workshops.

Other seniors like us have left long-term positions in their sixties only to search for—or be enticed back to—work after six, eight or twelve months. We left for a variety of reasons. Some took mandatory retirement, and others quit from boredom and exhaustion. Now we're returning for an equal variety of reasons: financial, social, intellectual or frequently some combination of all those aspects. Work, paid or volunteer, gives meaning and purpose to our lives. Work that we love helps us thrive. We've discovered that we are not yet ready to be put out—or to put ourselves out—to pasture.

My colleague Anne, a retired registered nurse and experienced health administrator, launched Elder Life Advocacy in the fall of 2010 after she found herself retired but restless. Her growing clientele attests to the desperate need for just such a service on Vancouver Island, and she is a fount of knowledge for seniors and their adult children. She bridges the generation gap and frequently the geographical gap as many seniors' adult children live far from their aging parents. Anne is still going strong in her seventies, a fierce advocate for the elderly.

Our generation grew up observing the virtues of volunteering. Helping out and reaching out are second nature to most of us. In fact all the many seniors I know are extremely busy, contributing generously in a multitude of ways to their communities. Volunteering keeps us young and engaged. It is our glowing light, illuminated by our own personal experience, that is most valuable to our family, friends and neighbours. Society needs our unique way of being in this world.

Eileen embodies genuine giving as a self-reliant, assertive, thriving ninety-two-year-old great-grandmother. She and her late husband, Bill, lived in a lovely two-bedroom condo in downtown Nanaimo, British Columbia. It was close to all the shopping she needed, one block away from a large theatre and near a long, level waterfront walkway. She regularly attended theatre performances and thoroughly enjoyed a daily walk along the waterfront. She and Bill were happy there for many years. They knew other people in the condo, and her daughters, grandchildren and friends regularly visited to bask in her joy and her generous-spirited, common-sense outlook on life. She listens, she laughs and she is always up for an adventure.

Bill died in the fall of 2003. Five years later Eileen was tired of living alone; she was particularly tired of making her own meals. She also wanted to make a move while she was still able to enjoy it. On her initiative she and her daughters checked out the local retirement residences, and she soon decided on the one with the best reputation for superb meals. When a sunny studio apartment became available, she quickly sold or gave away all her furniture and bought what she needed for her new downsized life. She never looked back.

Now Eileen is in her glory. She eats all her meals in the beautiful dining room and frequently invites friends or family to join her. Some of the residents are grumpy, resentful and withdrawn, but not the ones at her table. They're interesting to talk to and have much to share with guests. I've seen Eileen warmly reach out, introduce herself and welcome new arrivals to the residence. She enthusiastically participates in the many planned activities, including regular stretching exercises, aerobics for balance three times a week and twice-weekly canasta and cribbage. She just completed a quilt for her new great-grandson. She dresses up for Halloween and happily wears her pyjamas into the dining room for come-as-you-are pancake breakfasts. Staff members love her.

When her ninetieth birthday rolled around, her daughters and very close friends threw a big party. The invitation said, "Happy Birthday, Eileen. Still Dancing at Ninety." Eileen greets life with gusto and is an inspiration for us all. Age is no barrier to open-hearted giving, and passionate participation in life is a generous gift.

17

A WHOLEHEARTED LIFE

SEARCHING FOR JOY IS LIKE trying to pin jelly to a wall, but the place to begin is gratefulness. Nothing lifts a droopy day faster than thinking of a couple of things for which to be grateful, and there's always something, inside or out, that merits a heartfelt thank you. Have you ever noticed that when we're grateful, we immediately feel better? Joy is sure to follow. Gratefulness and joy inspire wholehearted living, which nurtures our spirit in a continuous unbroken loop.

In his book *Crossing the Unknown Sea: Work as a Pilgrimage of Identity*, David Whyte wrote of a life-changing conversation he had with his friend Brother David Steindl-Rast. At the time Whyte was feeling haunted, invisible and disconnected from himself and his work in the non-profit institute he had founded. Sharing a glass of wine with his friend, he said, "Tell me about exhaustion."

"You know the antidote to exhaustion is not necessarily rest?" Brother David said. "The antidote to exhaustion is wholeheartedness. . . . You are only half here, and half here will kill you after a while."

Wise words! We could all take these to heart when we grow weary after working and living half-heartedly or blindly pushing ourselves to be more and do more under the mistaken belief that we're just not working hard enough. I wish I'd heard both Davids' wisdom early in my career; it could have spared me trekking down many a blind alley. I was completely miscast as a student of economics, a toiling bookkeeper or a social worker.

But blind alleys do serve a purpose, if only to lead us to where we don't want to be and show us what doesn't work, thereby ensuring we keep on searching. Work as a pilgrimage of identity is something I never considered. It hadn't occurred to me that working wholeheartedly would be a clear indication that we are expressing our identity in the best way possible until I spent many years working wholeheartedly as a coach, counsellor and psychotherapist. The essence of our identity crystallizes with age and experience; how we express it will inevitably change. This keeps us energetically engaged and invigorated.

In his long white habit trimmed with black, David Steindl-Rast is tall, somewhat gaunt, regal and tranquil. As a Benedictine monk who studied with Buddhist masters, Brother David began writing and speaking in the mid-eighties about wholehearted living and gratefulness. His book *Gratefulness, the Heart of Prayer: An Approach to Life in Fullness*, released in 1984, launched a quiet revolution centred on living with gusto, gratefully and wholeheartedly.

The simple yet profound message in this book influences my life and the lives of thousands of others. I've never met Brother David, but I feel as though I know him. My then supervisor Emma introduced me to his wisdom within the grateful environment that permeated Hospice Victoria. She attended workshops that David offered in Washington state in the mid-eighties. Deeply touched by his message and his open-hearted sincerity, she gave me his tapes and recommended his book.

Since then I've viewed him on YouTube and explored his website, **www.gratefulness.org**. I never tire of hearing his rich, gentle voice or seeing his video clip *A Good Day*. It is an enchanting visual reminder that we have a world for which to be grateful. All we need do is wake up, open our eyes and look around, thankful we have eyes to open and ears that can hear, in fact thankful that we are alive!

Gratefulness is a choice, David teaches; it's a belief and a behaviour we can cultivate. It begins in the surprise and delight that accompanies gifts we receive. Every day as I walk I realize that our natural world is an endless gift. Prayer, as Steindl-Rast mentions in his book, is anything to which we bring the fullness of our attention, that is, anything we do with relish and gusto. Joy flows naturally from gratefulness, and together they produce wholeheartedness.

Wholeheartedness is contagious. On a cool, dark Sunday in November 2010, Lou and I attended the Island Soul Choir concert in Parksville, British Columbia. Brian Tate—an exuberant conductor, composer and musician—gathers together any adults who want to sing soul music and are willing to commit to memorizing all the music and attending five three-hour rehearsals between mid-August and the end of November. The choir has about a hundred members, approximately ninety women and ten men, and seniors make up about 70 per cent of the choir. The choir draws people from a wide geographic area; some travel many hours to attend rehearsals and end-of-season concerts.

All comers are welcome, including those who believe—because they were told so as children—they can't sing a note. Encouraged and included, new singers step out of the shadows to stand side by side with others who have the voice and stage presence of professionals. People in the audience frequently burst into clapping and finger-snapping or give voice to their own joy by singing along. The toe-tapping music, uplifting and heartfelt, is generously offered and received with gratitude.

When the applause died down, Brian turned to the audience and extended an open invitation to join the choir in January. His words certainly caught my attention, when it comes to singing: "There is safety in numbers. Your voice is welcome here."

When I cast around in my mind for an image of grateful, exuberant living, Anne Shirley of *Anne of Green Gables* fame comes readily to mind. No storybook heroine ever greeted life more wholeheartedly than Anne Shirley. She had a colourful imagination and a rapturous love of life born of her innate gratitude. She took nothing for granted, accustomed as she was to having her hopes and dreams dashed.

When I read Lucy Maud Montgomery's books as a young girl, I most admired Anne's courage and independent spirit. Like her I lived and breathed most freely out of doors in every season. There was always something exciting to do, and I particularly loved winter.

One year my brother and I worked like little Trojans under Dad's supervision as we cleared, levelled and flooded our backyard to make a skating rink. I was out there at every opportunity, shovelling snow or skating. The scar over my left eye, which required six stitches, dates from the time my friend Danny and I lifted the snow shovel too high and poked my eyebrow with the sharp corner.

Dad strung lights around the garage and back fence to light the rink in the dark days of winter. Mum made hot chocolate and Dad made his special french fries for all the neighbourhood kids. We had the only backyard skating rink around because my dad lovingly and wholeheartedly toiled to make it happen. Those were good days.

As an adult I feel an even closer kinship with Anne Shirley. The book on my shelf belonged to my mother and has an inscription: "To Margy, 1932." It has a faded, fir-green cloth cover and thick, yellowed pages reminiscent of rough cotton. The title is stamped on the front in old black script in the style of eighty years ago, and the binding is surprisingly still intact. I caress and turn the pages, chuckling at the exuberance of Anne's endless chatter. She was alive, awake to the exquisite details of her daily life. As I reread my Anne books, they inspire me and remind me that we can all rekindle our imagination, cultivate gratefulness and greet each new day wholeheartedly.

I am grateful for many things in my life, but most important are the people who have helped me along the way; you've met many of them in this book. In different ways and at different times these kind souls have all literally or metaphorically taken me by the hand and walked with me awhile. One of them was my first-year university English professor, William J. Goede; he reached out and touched a lost and confused young student. I remember Dr. Goede as a lanky, slightly stooped, intense man in a tweedy jacket that I suspect had leather patches on the elbows. His receding hairline made his long face longer still, and his spectacles covered piercing dark eyes softened by his innate kindness.

I was eighteen when I entered the University of Victoria in 1966 after reluctantly moving from Calgary with my mother and younger sister. I knew no one and barely scraped through my first year. One day that year Dr. Goede returned another poorly written and badly punctuated English paper along with a handwritten note on a piece of yellow paper—one of the few mementos I didn't destroy during my marathon shredding session a few years ago.

He was impressed by my clear-cut commitment to the things that count most in this world, he wrote, and added that these obviously didn't include punctuation. "In all things that matter most about this course—thinking new thoughts, questioning, fighting against the loss of liberty, and dehumanization—I put you clearly 'at the head of the class.' I think you will win in the dark night of the soul, regardless whether your enemy is ennui or the semicolon." It took me years to absorb the full meaning of his note; it carried me through many a dark night. He saw me more clearly than I saw myself and gave me something solid to grasp.

Our lives consist of such moments, and our personal philosophy provides a lens through which we view our experiences. We get to choose the lens, the memories to retain or discard and what now matters most.

Sailboat cruising anchors my life, as it has for more than forty years, and it has taught me valuable lessons: Embrace the journey, for it's how we navigate rough waters and calm seas that enriches our life. Storms always pass. Fog always lifts. Listen for the wind; it always arrives, frequently from an entirely unexpected direction. That's what makes life an ongoing adventure that we can choose to live with a whole and grateful heart.

Further reading

Albom, Mitch. *Tuesdays with Morrie: An Old Man, a Young Man, and Life's Greatest Lessons*. New York: Broadway Books, 1997.

Berkus, Rusty. *To Heal Again: Towards Serenity and the Resolution of Grief*. Los Angeles: Red Rose, 1986.

Bortz, Walter M. *We Live Too Short and Die Too Long: How to Achieve and Enjoy Your Natural 100-Year-Plus Life Span*. New York and Toronto: Bantam, 1991.

Boulanger, Gail. *Life Goes On: Losing, letting go and living again*. Nanoose Bay, BC: Notch Hill Books, 2012.

Callanan, Maggie. *Final Journeys: A Practical Guide for Bringing Care and Comfort at the End of Life*. New York and Toronto: Bantam, 2008.

Carson, Rachel. *The Sense of Wonder*. New York: Harper, 1998.

139

Chittister, Joan. *The Gift of Years; Growing Older Gracefully.* New York: BlueBridge, 2008.

Douglas, Gillean. *Silence Is My Homeland: Life on Teal River.* Whaletown, BC: Battle Maid Press, 2001.

Egoscue, Pete, with Roger Gittiness. *Pain Free: A Revolutionary Method for Stopping Chronic Pain.* New York: Bantam, 2000.

Ferrucci, Piero. *The Power of Kindness: The Unexpected Benefits of Leading a Compassionate Life.* New York: Tarcher, 2007.

Green, Lyndsay. *You Could Live a Long Time: Are You Ready?* Toronto: Thomas Allen, 2010.

Guarneri, Mimi. *The Heart Speaks: A Cardiologist Reveals the Secret Language of Healing.* New York: Touchstone, 2007.

Heilbrun, Carolyn G. *The Last Gift of Time: Life Beyond Sixty.* New York: Ballantine, 1997.

LeShan, Lawrence. *How to Meditate: A Guide to Self-Discovery.* Boston: Bantam, 1975.

Nelson, Miriam E., with Sarah Wernick. *Strong Women Stay Young.* New York and Toronto: Bantam, 1997.

Pausch, Randy, with Jeffrey Zaslow. *The Last Lecture.* New York: Hyperion, 2008.

Rupp, Joyce. *Walk in a Relaxed Manner: Life Lessons from the Camino.* New York: Orbis Books, 2005.

Schachter-Shalomi, Zalman, and Ronald S. Miller. *From Age-ing to Sage-ing: A Profound New Vision of Growing Older.* New York: Warner Books, 1997.

Schwartz, Morrie. *Morrie in His Own Words: Life Wisdom from a Remarkable Man.* New York: Walker Publishing Company, Inc., 1996.

Sher, Gail. *One Continuous Mistake: Four Noble Truths for Writers.* New York: Penguin Compass, 1999.

Steindl-Rast, David. *Gratefulness, the Heart of Prayer: An Approach to Life in Fullness.* New York: Paulist Press, 1984.

Taylor, Jill Bolte. *My Stroke of Insight: A Brain Scientist's Personal Journey.* New York: Viking Penguin, 2006.

Whyte, David. *Crossing the Unknown Sea: Work as a Pilgrimage of Identity.* New York: Riverhead Books, 2001.

About the author

Gail Boulanger spent twenty-five years as a coach, counsellor, consultant, and psychotherapist. She is the author of *Life Goes On: Losing, letting go and living again* (2002), republished in 2012. It is a practical book about how to gently and effectively navigate our way through all types of grief and loss. Gail now offers coaching and counselling for vibrant living from her office in Nanoose Bay on Vancouver Island. She holds a BA in Psychology and an MA in Counselling Psychology. Her favourite pastimes are writing, walking, baking cookies and sailing.

Visit the author online at **www.gailboulanger.com**.